S0-EFN-369

Illustrated History of Women

VOLUME 10

A New Wave:
1960–1998

Irene M. Franck

David M. Brownstone

Grolier Educational

How to Use This Book

A New Wave: 1960–1998 is Volume 10 of the *Illustrated History of Women*. This set covers the story of women from the earliest times to today, in ten volumes (listed on the back cover).

To find articles that interest you, you can start by looking at the Table of Contents given at the front of each book. Volume 1, set in the earliest times, is organized by culture. In Volumes 2–10, the contents are divided into four general sections: Religion, Education, and Everyday Life; Political Life; Science, Technology, and Medicine; and Arts and Literature.

To find discussion of specific topics and people, you can also look in the Master Index. This is repeated at the end of each volume.

For a general introduction to the period covered, look at the Overview at the front of each volume. Following the Overview, you will also find a Timeline, a brief chronology of key events in that period.

For more on women's history, look at Further Reading on Women's History, a list of general books, given on page 104 of Volume 1. At the end of each volume, you will also find a list of books relating to the specific period covered. Tips for online research are given in Women's History on the Internet on page 112 of Volume 3.

First published in the United States in 1999 by Grolier Educational,
Sherman Turnpike, Danbury, CT 06816

Copyright © 1999 by Irene M. Franck and David M. Brownstone

When referencing this publication, use the following citation:
Franck, Irene M., and David M. Brownstone. *Illustrated History of Women,* 10 volumes, Danbury, CT: Grolier Educational, 1999.

Illustration credits for all 10 volumes of the *Illustrated History of Women* are given on pages 111-112 of Volume 1.

Library of Congress Cataloging-in-Publication Data
Franck, Irene M.
    Illustrated History of Women
    Irene M. Franck and David M. Brownstone
        p.   cm.
    Includes bibliographical references (p.) and index.
    Contents: v.1. Early times, from prehistory to 499 A.D.—v. 2. Between darkness and dawn, 500-1399—v.3. Emerging into the light, 1400-1599—v.4. Troubled times, 1500-1749—v. 5. Age of revolution, 1750-1829—v.6. Dawn of a new age, 1830-1869—v.7. Opening doors, 1870-1899—v.8. Winning through, 1900-1929—v.9. Depression and war, 1930-1959—v.10. A new wave, 1960-1998.
    Summary: Presents a history of women around the world from earliest times to the present day.
    ISBN 0-7172-7497-7 (hard: set:alk.paper).—ISBN 0-7172-9255-X (hard: v.1: alk. paper).—ISBN 0-7172-9256-8 (hard: v.2: alk. paper).—ISBN 0-7172-9257-6 (hard: v.3: alk. paper).—ISBN 0-7172-9258-4 (hard: v.4: alk. paper).—ISBN 0-7172-9259-2 (hard: v.5: alk. paper).—ISBN 0-7172-9260-6 (hard: v.6: alk. paper).—ISBN 0-7172-9261-4 (hard: v.7: alk. paper).—ISBN 0-7172-9262-2 (hard: v.8: alk. paper).—ISBN 0-7172-9263-0 (hard: v.9: alk. paper).—ISBN 0-7172-9264-9(hard: v.10: alk. paper).
    1. Women—History—Juvenile literature. 2. Women—History-Chronology—Juvenile literature. [1. Women—History.]
    HQ1121.I45 1998
    305.4'09—dc21   98-44318
                                                                                          CIP
                                                                                          AC

Printed in the United States of America
Designed by Combined Publishing

Contents

How to Use This Book   2

Overview: 1960–1998   5

Timeline: 1960–1998   7

Political Life   9

  Women, Power, and Politics   10

    Highlights in the Modern Fight for Women's Political Rights   18

  Women and Civil Rights   22

    Fannie Lou Hamer   25

  War and Peace   26

  The New Women's Rights Movement   32

    Betty Friedan   34

    The Equal Rights Amendment   38

Religion, Education, and Everyday Life   41

  Changing Lives   42

  Women at Work   47

    Anita Faye Hill and Clarence Thomas   52

  Women in the News   54

  Women in Education   56

  Women in Religion   59

  Flying High   62

  Changing Styles   66

  Women in Sports   70

Science, Technology, and Medicine   77

    Women's Bodies, Women's Lives   78

       Roe v. Wade   82

    Women in Science   84

    Rachel Carson and the Green Movement   87

Arts and Literature   89

    Writing Women   90

    On Stage and Screen   96

    Music and Dance   103

    Visual Arts   110

Further Reading: 1960–1998   112

Master Index   113

Overview: 1960–1998

In the 1960s and beyond, a second 20th-century dawn came for the world's women, as they explored both old and new women's rights issues. Betty Friedan led the way in the "new wave" of the women's movement with *The Feminine Mystique*, and with her cofounding of the National Organization for Women (NOW) in the United States.

In this period, there also emerged a wide range of new leaders, who quite naturally went far beyond women's rights issues to take up all the matters facing humanity. Rachel Carson led the way on the chemical poisoning of the environment, with her book *Silent Spring*, and many other women across the world would take up the dangers facing humanity, especially in the nuclear age. In Sri Lanka, Sirimavo Bandaranaike became the world's first elected woman prime minister. She would be followed by Indira Gandhi, Margaret Thatcher, Benazir Bhutto, and hundreds of other politicians. Together they brought women into the full range of the world's leadership—though at century's end there would still be far too few women in the world's top political, economic, and military leadership positions.

In these decades, women continued to expand their roles in the world of entertainment—though, again, with far too few in the top industry positions. Major women stars were known around the world, for their faces appeared on hundreds of millions of movie and television screens. Added to this were many new international women sports celebrities, as the audience for such activities expanded with the spread of television.

In every other area, women moved forward as well. As writers, artists, scientists, business leaders, and all the rest, they became a major force in the development of the world. Even so, women still faced discrimination at all levels of society, and in some regions were being forced out of any roles except that of homemaker. With the 21st century approaching, women's lives were still changing, while the long drive for equality and freedom continued.

For an outline of key events in this period, see "Timeline: 1960–1998" (p. 7).

Timeline: 1960–1998

1960

Earth's population was up to an estimated 3 billion–3.1 billion.

John Fitzgerald Kennedy became the 35th president of the United States.

1961

Soviet cosmonaut Yuri Gagarin was the first person to orbit the Earth, in *Vostok I.*

1962

The Cuban Missile Crisis came very close to triggering thermonuclear war.

Rachel Carson published *Silent Spring,* on chemical pollution of the world's environment.

1963

Martin Luther King, Jr., led a massive desegregation campaign in Birmingham, Alabama.

President John Fitzgerald Kennedy was assassinated in Dallas, Texas (Nov. 22). Lyndon B. Johnson became the 36th president.

1964

Major U.S. forces were committed to the Vietnam War.

U.S. president Lyndon B. Johnson was elected in his own right.

The Civil Rights Act made a wide range of discrimination illegal.

1965

India defeated Pakistan in the second India-Pakistan War.

1965

Race riots destroyed much the Watts district of Los Angeles; 35 people died.

1966

Mao Zedong initiated China's destructive and failed Cultural Revolution (1966–1969).

Race riots scarred many U.S. cities, including Detroit, Chicago, and New York.

1967

Detroit race riots killed 43 people, while 26 died in Newark.

Israel defeated its neighbors in the Six-Day War (Third Arab-Israeli War).

1968

Richard M. Nixon became the 37th president of the United States.

Martin Luther King, Jr., and Robert Francis Kennedy were assassinated.

Soviet invasion forces destroyed the new Czech democracy (Prague Spring).

1969

U.S. astronauts Neil Armstrong and Edwin Aldrin landed on the moon.

Some 400,000 people gathered at the Woodstock, New York, music festival.

1970

National Guard troops fired on unarmed antiwar protesters at Kent State University, killing four.

1972

The Watergate scandal began with a Republican break-in at the Democratic National Committee headquarters.

The deadly pesticide DDT was banned in the U.S.

1973

Richard M. Nixon began his second term as U.S. president.

The Paris Peace Accords ended the Vietnam War.

Israel won the Yom Kippur War (Fourth Arab-Israeli War).

1974

Richard M. Nixon resigned his presidency to avoid impeachment in the Watergate scandal. Gerald Ford became the 38th president.

1975

Australia's Great Barrier Reef became the world's largest marine protected area.

1976

Chinese Communist leaders Mao Zedong, Zhou Enlai, and Zhu De died, all of natural causes.

1977

Jimmy Carter became the 39th President of the United States.

1978
Egypt's Anwar el-Sadat and Israel's Menachem Begin signed the Camp David Accords, bringing Egyptian-Israeli peace closer.

1979
Soviet forces intervened in the Afghan Civil War.

1981
Ronald Reagan became the 40th president of the United States.

AIDS (acquired immunodeficiency syndrome) was recognized as a disease.

Egyptian premier Anwar el-Sadat was assassinated by Islamic fundamentalists in Cairo.

1982
Israeli forces invaded Lebanon, withdrawing in 1983, after the Sabra and Shatilla refugee camp murders.

1983
In Iran's Nowruz oil field, a well blowout and Iraqi attacks created the world's worst oil spill so far.

1984
Indian prime minister Indira Gandhi was assassinated, by two members of her Sikh bodyguard.

1985
Mikhail Gorbachev became leader of the Soviet Union, instituting major political and economic changes that ultimately caused the Soviet state to dissolve.

Ronald Reagan began his second term as U.S. president.

1986
At Chernobyl, near Kiev, in Ukraine, world's worst nuclear accident occurred.

1987
Ronald Reagan and Mikhail Gorbachev agreed on the Intermediate Nuclear Forces (INF) Treaty; the nuclear war threat lessened.

1988
The Geneva Agreement ended the Afghan-Soviet War.

1989
George Bush became the 41st president of the United States.

Chinese troops massacred hundreds of pro-democracy demonstrators at Beijing's Tienanmen Square.

Czechoslovakia, Poland, and East Germany threw off their Communist governments.

1990
Iraqi forces took Kuwait, beginning the Persian Gulf War.

1991
Allied forces smashed the Iraqi army, ending the Persian Gulf War.

The Soviet Union dissolved, following a Communist coup attempt.

1993
Bill Clinton became the 42nd president of the United States.

Russian government forces defeated a parliament-supported rising in Moscow.

1994
Israeli-Palestinian peace accords were signed. The Palestinian National Authority was established.

Hutu extremists murdered 500,000–1 million Tutsis in Rwanda.

1995
The Bosnian War ended with the partition of Bosnia between the Bosnian-Croatian alliance and the Serbian republic.

Israeli prime minister Yitzhak Rabin was assassinated.

1997
Bill Clinton began his second term as U.S. president.

Economic crises struck Indonesia, Malaysia, Thailand, and Korea.

1998
New accords brought a fragile peace to Northern Ireland.

India and Pakistan tested their first nuclear weapons.

Financial crises worsened in Southeast Asia, Japan, and Russia.

Illustrated History of Women

Political Life

Women, Power, and Politics

In the 1960s, breakthroughs began to come. Although most of women's major battles for equality still remained to be won, suddenly there were elected women prime ministers in major countries, where before there had been none. Beyond that, there were women in all kinds of other high positions from which they previously had been barred.

In 1960, Sirimavo Bandaranaike (1916–) became the world's first woman prime minister, in Sri Lanka. Her husband, Sri Lankan prime minister Solomon Bandaranaike, had been assassinated in 1959. She succeeded him, serving until 1965, and then again from 1970 to 1977. Her daughter, Chandrika Bandaranaike Kumaratunga (1946–), became prime minister of Sri Lanka in 1994.

Above: *Queen Elizabeth II symbolized Britain and the Commonwealth for many people around the world, though political power was now held primarily by Parliament.*

From 1966 until her assassination in 1984, Indira Gandhi was either prime minister of India or a major opposition figure.

Conservative Party leader Margaret Thatcher became Britain's longest-serving prime minister in the 20th century.

The ability of women to make it to the top of their political systems, lead successfully, and be returned to office again and again was made completely clear by British prime minister Margaret Thatcher (1925–). Far from being any other leader's daughter, wife, or political heir—and very far from being a feminist, leading women's rights advocate, or even mild liberal—Thatcher was the arch-conservative leader of Britain's Conservative Party. Thatcher chose to lead her country as a practical right-wing politician with views a great deal less feminist than many men in politics, becoming the longest-serving British prime minister of the 20th century (1979–1990).

Yet another woman politician who became a great world figure was Aung San Suu Kyi (1945–), a human rights leader

She was still serving in that post in late 1998, while her country remained gripped by the long Sri Lankan Civil War (1981–).

A second major major breakthrough to power, this one huge, came in 1966, with the election of Indira Gandhi (1917–1984) as prime minister of India, the world's largest democracy—and the country with the world's second-largest population. Gandhi was the daughter of Jawaharlal Nehru, the first prime minister of independent India. However, hundreds of millions of Indians elected and reelected her on her own, settling once and for all the question of whether a woman could be elected and lead a major country. It was then only a question of time before women would be leading many countries.

Aung San Suu Kyi became the leader of the movement opposing the army dictatorship of Myanmar (formerly Burma).

from Myanmar (formerly Burma), who was awarded the 1991 Nobel Peace Prize. She is the daughter of Aung San (1914–1947), the founder and first prime minister of modern Burma, who was assassinated in 1947. After living abroad from 1960, she returned to Myanmar in 1988 to nurse her sick mother, and was soon swept into politics, as leader of the nonviolent democratic forces opposing the military dictatorship. A short-lived democratic government was crushed by the military in 1988, but she remained in Myanmar and in the fight for democracy. Though kept under house ar-

In and out of office, Pakistani leader Benazir Bhutto had major battles with army and fundamentalist leaders.

rest by the military for six years, she won Myanmar's 1990 elections, which the military refused to honor. She was formally released in 1995, though with her freedom still severely limited, and continued to lead her country's freedom movement, while the world feared for her safety.

A similar course—though with very different results—was taken by Philippines democratic leader Corazon Cojuangco Aquino (1933–). Her husband, Benigno Aquino, had been assassinated on his return from exile in 1983 by agents of Philippines dictator Ferdinand Marcos. She

Corazon Aquino led a popular revolution to oust Philippines dictator Ferdinand Marcos, after he tried to set aside a democratic election that her party had won, in 1986.

POLITICAL LIFE

succeeded him as head of her country's Liberal Party in 1983 and went on to defeat Marcos in the 1986 Philippines presidential election. Though Marcos attempted to steal the election by fraud and military force, she led the fight against Marcos, who fled the country. Defeating six antidemocratic coup attempts while in office (1986–1992), Aquino was able to set her country back on the path of democracy.

Benazir Bhutto (1942–) was another member of a political family who moved into power. Her father, Zulfikar Ali Bhutto, had been prime minister of Pakistan (1972–1977) until deposed by an army coup, and had been executed in 1979 on a false murder charge. Benazir Bhutto returned to Pakistan in 1986 to lead the opposition to Mohammad Zia Ul-Haq's military government. After Zia's death in a plane crash in 1988, she was elected prime minister of Pakistan. In office, she became one of the world's leading women, despite continuing army and religious fundamentalist opposition at home. Removed from office in 1990, and defeated in elections later that year, she scored a massive comeback victory in 1993, serving as prime minister until removed again in 1996.

Jiang Qing (Luan Shu-meng; 1914–1991) was another Asian woman leader who made a strong drive toward national power,

Jiang Qing (before microphones) was a powerful figure in China when her husband, Mao Zedong, was alive. After his death she was tried for taking power illegally and imprisoned.

but in her instance it failed. Jiang began her career as an actress (stage name Lan P'ing), but she rose to great power as the third wife of Chinese Communist leader Mao Zedong. From 1966 until his death in 1976, she was second only to Mao in China, as the active leader of the hugely destructive Cultural Revolution, which smashed much of China's culture and society. After Mao's death, she quickly lost power. China's new, more moderate Communist rulers accused her of trying to take power illegally, as leader of the "Gang of Four." She died in prison.

Tansu Çiller was the first woman to become prime minister of an Islamic country, Turkey, on her own, without having a family link to power.

Golda Meir was the first woman to become prime minister of Israel, serving from 1969 to 1974.

Many other women also came to power throughout the world in the late 20th century. One of the most notable of these was Golda Meir (1898–1978), the first woman to become prime minister of Israel (1969–1974). Another was Norwegian physician Gro Harlem Brundtland (1939–), who became her country's long-serving (and first woman) prime minister (1981–1996). A third was Tansu Çiller (1946–), Turkey's first woman prime minister (1993–1995). She was especially notable as the first woman to lead an Islamic country without a family link to power.

Betty Boothroyd posed in her robes of office after becoming the first woman Speaker of Britain's Parliament in 1992.

In Argentina, Vice President Isabelita Perón, President Juan Perón's second wife, succeeded him to the presidency after his death in 1974, and ruled the country for two years (1974–1976). She was overthrown by a coup in 1976, and then imprisoned for five years (1976–1981). Perón's first wife, Maria Eva "Evita" Perón had been an extraordinarily popular figure (see "Building a New World," Vol. 9, p. 25).

In Central America, Violeta Chamorro (1939–) became president of Nicaragua in 1990, negotiating the end of the Nicaraguan Civil War that year. Farther north, in Canada, Kim Campbell became her country's first woman prime minister (1993).

In Britain, Shirley Brittain Williams was cofounder of Britain's Social Democratic Party (1981), and Betty Boothroyd was the first woman to become Speaker of Parliament (1992). Across the Irish Sea, Mary Bourke Robinson became the first woman president of Ireland (1990), while across the English Channel, Edith Cresson became the first woman prime minister of France (1991).

Mary Robinson was the first woman to become president of Ireland, in 1990.

Sandra Day O'Connor was the first woman on the U.S. Supreme Court, appointed as an associate justice in 1981.

In Germany, Ulrike Meinhof was a leader of the anarchist-terrorist Red Army Faction (Baader-Meinhof Group) in the early 1970s. Later in that decade Petra Kelly founded Germany's environmentalist Green Party (1979).

The United States

As in many other countries, in the United States women—with a wide range of political and social views—moved into politics, government, and law in large numbers in the late 20th century. One very notable example is Arizona lawyer and politician Sandra Day O'Connor (1930–). In 1981 President Ronald Reagan appointed her to be the first woman associate justice of the U.S. Supreme Court—a landmark breakthrough for American women. Before joining the Court, O'Connor had been a prosecutor, state senator, and judge.

The Supreme Court's second woman member came in 1993, with President Bill Clinton's appointment of lawyer and law professor Ruth Bader Ginsburg (1933–).

Ruth Bader Ginsburg, a women's rights advocate, was the second woman named to the U.S. Supreme Court, in 1993.

A nationally known lawyer in her own right, Hillary Rodham Clinton became an enormously active and influential first lady after 1993, when her husband, Bill Clinton, became U.S. president.

Earlier in her career, Ginsburg had won several major women's rights cases in arguments before the Supreme Court. In the late 1960s and early 1970s, she headed the American Civil Liberties Union Women's Rights Project.

Another notable woman in the law was Hillary Rodham Clinton (1947–), a trial lawyer and law professor, who had chaired the American Bar Association Commission on Women in the Professions. She became a world figure in 1993, however, as a very unusual first lady, taking a much larger and more direct part in politics than ever before. Eleanor Roosevelt had strongly participated in politics, but never directly "carried the ball" on specific issues, as Hillary Clinton did for the national health care campaign during President Bill Clinton's first term. That campaign was lost, however, and she later took a less direct role. She also was

Madeleine Albright was U.S. ambassador to the United Nations before she became the first woman secretary of state in 1997.

the focus of Republican attacks on the Whitewater issue, even becoming the only first lady ever to testify before a grand jury.

An American first lady who had taken an entirely different tack while living in the White House was Jacqueline Bouvier Kennedy (later Onassis; 1929–1994). She had married John Fitzgerald Kennedy, then a senator, in 1953, and moved into the White House with him in 1961. During her nearly three years as first lady, "Jackie" Kennedy was—like most first ladies—not at all involved directly in politics, but instead was a worldwide social and fashion figure. With President Kennedy's 1963 assassination, she became the revered widow of a great

Hazel O'Leary was U.S. secretary of energy in the Clinton administration, the first to have actually worked in the industry before taking office, as an energy consultant and executive.

Carol Moseley Braun was the first African-American woman in the U.S. Senate, in 1993.

American hero, with a unique place in the American history of her time, for as long as she lived.

These were just a few of the many women moving into power around the world. For some others, including some notable "firsts," see "Highlights in the Modern Fight for Women's Political Rights," below. Many other women were active in the fight for civil rights (see p. 22). Among them were Winnie Mandela and Fannie Lou Hamer (see p. 25). Many others were working for women's rights (see p. 32) and dealing with questions of war and peace (see p. 26).

Highlights in the Modern Fight for Women's Political Rights

1944

Hattie Ophelia Wyatt Caraway ended her 13 years in the U.S. Senate as a Democrat from Arkansas. The first woman in the Senate, replacing her husband, Thaddeus Caraway, at his death in 1931, she was also the first elected to the Senate, in 1932.

1946

The United Nations Commission on the Status of Women was formed.

1948

Eleanor Roosevelt chaired the United Nations Commission on Human Rights, which passed the landmark UN Declaration of Human Rights.

1949

The Second Sex, a centerpiece of feminist thinking, was published by Simone de Beauvoir.

Georgia Neese Clark Gray was the first woman to be treasurer of the United States.

1960

Sirimavo Bandaranaike became the world's first woman prime minister, in Sri Lanka.

Margaret Chase Smith won her third term in Maine, in the first all-woman U.S. Senate race.

1961

The President's Commission on the Status of Women was established, led by Eleanor Roosevelt and Esther Peterson.

1963

The Feminine Mystique, a key work in the modern American women's movement, was published by Betty Friedan.

The Equal Pay Act, the first federal law against sexual discrimination, was passed by the U.S. Congress.

1964

Marietta Tree was the first woman to become permanent U.S. ambassador to the United Nations; three years earlier, she had been the first to be chief U.S. delegate.

The U.S. Congress passed Title VII of the Civil Rights Act prohibiting employment discrimination based on race, color, religion, sex, or national origin, and creating the Equal Employment Opportunity Commission (EEOC).

1966

The National Organization for Women was founded, with Betty Friedan as president.

Indira Gandhi became the first woman prime minister of India.

Constance Baker Motley was the first African-American woman to be appointed a U.S. federal judge.

1967

The International Declaration on the Elimination of Discrimination Against Women was passed.

1969

Golda Meir became the first woman prime minister of Israel.

Shirley Chisholm was the first African-American woman to be elected to the U.S. House of Representatives.

1971

Helga Pedersen became the first woman judge on the European Court of Human Rights.

Ms. magazine was established by a group of feminist writers, including its first editor, Gloria Steinem.

The U.S. House of Representatives passed the Equal Rights Amendment (ERA), as did the Senate a year later, but it would fail to be ratified (1982).

1972

The U.S. Congress passed Title IX of the Educational Amendments Act, barring discrimination on the basis of sex in all public undergraduate schools and in most private and public graduate and vocational schools that receive public funds.

Anne L. Armstrong became the first woman to deliver the keynote speech at a major party's national convention, for the Republicans.

1973

In *Roe v. Wade*, the U.S. Supreme Court for the first time legalized abortion in the United States.

1974

The U.S. Merchant Marine Academy became the first of the American service academies to admit women. The others would follow in 1976.

Ella Grasso became the first woman to be elected governor of a state on her own, not succeeding her husband, in Connecticut.

1975

Margaret Thatcher became the first woman to lead a major British political party, the Conservative Party, later becoming her country's longest-serving 20th-century prime minister (1979–1990).

The Equal Credit Opportunity Act was passed by the U.S. Congress, from 1977 prohibiting creditor discrimination on the basis of race, ethnic origin, religion, age, sex, marital status, or welfare status.

The International Women's Year and the United Nations Decade for Women: Equality, Development, Peace, both began with the World Conference on Women in Mexico City.

1978

The Women's Armed Forces Integration Act was passed, integrating women into the U.S. armed forces.

Nancy Landon Kassebaum was the first woman to be elected U.S. senator on her own, not as the wife of a former congressman, from Kansas.

1979

The United Nations General Assembly adopted the Convention on the Elimination of All Forms of Discrimination Against Women.

1980

The Women's Rights National Historic Park was established in Seneca Falls, New York.

Vigdis Finnbogadottir became the first woman president of Iceland.

1981

Sandra Day O'Connor was the first woman appointed to the U.S. Supreme Court.

Gro Harlem Brundtland became the first woman prime minister of Norway.

1983

Jeanne Sauvé became the first woman governor general of Canada.

1984

Geraldine Ferraro was the first woman to be a vice-presidential candidate for a major United States political party, the Democrats, as the running mate of losing candidate Walter Mondale.

1985

Wilma P. Mankiller was elected chief of the Cherokee, the first woman elected to be chief of a major Native-American people.

1986

Corazon Aquino became president of the Philippines, the first woman in the post, after the Philippine Revolution upheld her election.

Takako Doi was the first woman to be elected leader of a major Japanese political party, the Socialist Party.

1987

Susan Estrich was the first woman to manage a presidential campaign for a major U.S. political party, the Democrats.

Elizabeth Havers Butler-Sloss was the first woman appointed to Britain's Court of Appeal.

1988

Benazir Bhutto became the first woman prime minister of Pakistan.

1990

Mary Bourke Robinson became the first woman president of Ireland.

1991

Anita Faye Hill charged Supreme Court nominee Clarence Thomas with sexual harassment in internationally televised hearings, revitalizing the women's movement.

Aung San Suu Kyi won the Nobel Peace Prize for her activities as leader of the opposition against the military dictatorship of Myanmar (Burma).

Edith Cresson became the first woman prime minister of France.

1992

In the "Year of the Woman," Carol Moseley Braun became the first African-American woman elected to the U.S. Senate, from Illinois, and California became the first state to elect two women to the Senate: Dianne Feinstein and Barbara Boxer. Patty Murray from Washington was elected as well, joining Barbara Mikulski, a senator from Maryland since 1986, and Nancy Kassebaum, a senator from Kansas since 1979.

Betty Boothroyd was elected the first woman Speaker of Britain's Parliament.

1993

Tansu Çiller became the first woman prime minister of Turkey and the first woman to lead an Islamic country on her own, not as part of a family succession.

Janet Reno was the first woman to become U.S. attorney general.

Sheila Evans Widnall became the first woman secretary of the air force.

Kim Campbell became the first woman prime minister of Canada.

1994

Chandrika Bandaranaike Kumaratunga was elected prime minister of Sri Lanka.

1997

Madeleine Albright was the first woman to become U.S. secretary of state.

1998

Ruth Dreifuss was the first woman (and the first Jew) to become the president of Switzerland.

Janet Reno

(See also "Key Events in the Early Fight for Women's Rights," Vol. 8, p. 18 and "Women and the Vote," Vol. 8, p. 13.)

Women and Civil Rights

The late 20th century saw some major movements toward winning civil rights for all. The two most notable were in the United States and South Africa, with women heavily involved in both.

U.S. Civil Rights Movement

The modern U.S. civil rights movement had started in the mid-1950s (see "Building a New World," Vol. 9, p. 25), but it grew into a massive, connected set of nationwide movements in the 1960s and 1970s. After Rosa Parks came hundreds and thousands of strong, effective, dedicated women who worked in the cause of civil rights. One of them was Fannie Lou Hamer (see p. 25). Coretta Scott King (1922–) worked alongside her husband, Martin Luther King, Jr., in the early civil rights movement, continuing in the work after his 1968 assassination.

Shirley Chisholm was a trailblazing African-American political leader. A Democrat from New York, she became the first Black woman member of the U.S. House of Representatives (1969–1983). She also ran for the Democratic nomination for president in 1972. In 1993, 24 years later, Carol Moseley Braun (1947–), a Democrat from Illinois, was the first African-American woman to become a U.S. senator.

Another major figure who emerged during the modern battle for civil rights was lawyer and politician Barbara Charlene Jordan (1936–1996). She was the first African-American Texas state legislator (1966–1972) since the Reconstruction period, after the Civil War. She went on to serve in U.S. Con-

Above: *After the 1968 assassination of her husband, civil rights leader Martin Luther King, Jr., Coretta Scott King founded the Martin Luther King Memorial Center, to continue his work.*

gress (1973–1979) and was a celebrated keynote speaker at the 1976 Democratic National Convention.

Myrlie Evers-Williams (1933–) also emerged from the civil rights struggle, becoming a major figure in the 1990s. She was the wife of Medgar Evers, Mississippi leader of the National Association for the Advancement of Colored People (NAACP), who was murdered by racist Byron De La Beckwith in 1963. She then began a 31-year-long campaign to have De La Beckwith con-

Longtime civil rights lawyer Constance Baker Motley was the first African-American woman to be a federal judge, appointed by President Lyndon Johnson (right).

victed of her husband's murder, finally succeeding in 1994. In the course of her long campaign, she became a major civil rights figure, paving the way for her election as chairwoman of the NAACP in 1995.

South Africa

In South Africa, the policy of absolute racial separation—called *apartheid*—had been made law in 1948. The whole world watched as the South African government tried to smash all who opposed its racist policies, imprisoning many freedom movement leaders, most notably Nelson Mandela for 28 years (1962–1990). Democracy finally came, in 1993, after a long and often bloody struggle involving millions of South Africans of many races and ethnic groups.

Shirley Chisholm was the first African-American woman in the U.S. House of Representatives, in 1969, and ran for the Democratic presidential nomination in 1972.

Winnie Mandela was a key figure in the fight against apartheid in South Africa, as a leader in the African National Congress and (until 1995) the wife of Nelson Mandela.

Winnie Nomzano Mandela (1934–) was the leading woman in the South African freedom movement, as the wife of Nelson Mandela and on her own. The government denied her the right to speak for many years, and forced her into internal exile in 1977, far from the country's main centers. Even so, she found ways to make herself heard. Later, however, after freedom was achieved, she ran into many difficulties, including the end of her marriage to Nelson Mandela.

Other women were also notable anti-apartheid activists. An early leader was Lilian Ngoyi (1911–1980), president of the African National Congress Women's League (1953) and the Federation of South

African Women (1956). Notsikelelo Albertina Sisulu (1919–) was another key leader in the African National Congress and other antiapartheid organizations. So was Fatima Meer (1929–), president of the Black Women's Federation (1975).

White South African women also played a key role in the fight. Helen Gavronsky Suzman (1917–) cofounded the antiapartheid Progressive Party (1959), and was for many years its only member in Parliament. She was given the United Nations Human

A leader of South Africa's Progressive Party, Helen Suzman was praised around the world for her work against the racist apartheid system.

POLITICAL LIFE

Fannie Lou Hamer

One of the most effective political women in the United States civil rights movement was African-American politician Fannie Lou Hamer (1917–1977). She led the tremendously important fight to break the seating pattern that favored White segregationist delegates, excluding Black delegates, from the South at the Democratic National Convention.

A Mississippi sharecropper, Hamer was a founder of the Mississippi Freedom Democratic Party. Her party challenged the seating of the racist regular Mississippi delegation at the 1964 Democratic National Convention and again in 1968, both times without success. In 1972, however, her party scored a major civil rights victory when it blocked the seating of the racist delegates, with the Mississippi Freedom Democratic Party's pro–civil rights delegates seated in their place. Racist delegates were then challenged from many states, and the national Democratic Party swung sharply toward the pro–civil rights position. In leading that fight, Hamer made a major and lasting contribution to the civil rights cause.

Fannie Lou Hamer led the fight to open the Democratic National Convention to African-American delegates from the South. Here she was testifying at the convention in 1964.

Rights Award in 1978. An earlier parliamentary figure was Margaret Hodgson Ballinger (1894–1980), who founded the Liberal Party (1953). Helen Pennell Joseph (1905–1992) was imprisoned more than once for her antiapartheid activities. Ruth First (1925–1982), a member of the South African Communist Party and African National Congress, was killed by a letter bomb, in the sometimes violent campaign.

War and Peace

As all sane people know, war is a great evil. As is also perfectly clear, war continues to be one of humanity's chief occupations; indeed, a whole series of occupations going far beyond the purely military.

So it is that many of the world's best and most notable women have long gone about the business of trying to prevent war and to end wars in being. These are the women who help create and build antiwar movements, trying to make war itself unthinkable.

So it is also that millions of the world's women—who generally like war no better than women in peace movements—continue to try to break into, move up in, and go to the top of the world's male-dominated mili-

Above: Despite the hazards of political protests in the Soviet Union at the time, these Soviet women physicians and nurses were protesting against the nuclear arms race in 1984.

A founder of Germany's environmentalist Green Party, Petra Kelly was here being arrested during an antinuclear protest at the U.S. missile base in Stuttgart in 1985.

Jeanne Holm helped open the U.S. Air Force to women, becoming its first woman brigadier general and retiring as a major general.

tary occupations, all the way to frontline combat and top command positions.

The Nuclear Threat

One of the greatest of all issues in the 20th century has been that of nuclear weapons. Despite the end of the Cold War, the existence and spread of nuclear weapons continues to threaten humanity and all other life on Earth. It is unclear who has made the greatest contribution toward even the small control of these weapons achieved so far. People in peace movements continue to try to build anti-bomb campaigns. On the other hand, many political figures who have

negotiated for arms control argue that control can only be gained from strength. Among the latter are former British prime minister Margaret Thatcher and U.S. secretary of state Madeleine Albright (see "Women, Power, and Politics," p. 10).

Many women in peace movements have been greatly active in ban-the-bomb activities. One of the most notable is Helen Broinowski Caldicott (1938–). An Australian pediatrician, Caldicott's life was changed by reading Nevil Shute's 1957 novel *On the Beach* (basis for the 1959 film). The fictional story was set in Australia after a nuclear war, where the remnants of humanity await the arrival of the nuclear cloud that is spreading and destroying all life on earth. Caldicott inspired a substantial antinuclear campaign in Australia and the South Pacific, which contributed to the growth of major antinuclear campaigns in that part of the world in the 1980s and 1990s. In 1977, she became a major figure in Physicians for Social Responsibility, and later founded Women's Action for Nuclear Disarmament.

Two other key U.S. anti-bomb campaigners were Bella Abzug and Dagmar Wilson. In 1960 they founded Women Strike for Peace, an organization that campaigned for nuclear disarmament along with such other organizations as the Women's International League for Peace and Freedom and the Committee for a Sane Nuclear Policy. In the late 1960s, Women Strike for Peace and many other anti-bomb groups also became opponents of U.S. participation in the Vietnam War.

In what was then the Soviet Union, women and men were far less free to cam-

Many women supported the often-violent attempts to end British control of Northern Ireland, like the protesters here, but many others sought peace in the troubled region.

paign against nuclear weapons testing than in the West, as they and all other dissidents faced very real danger of imprisonment and exile. One very notable antinuclear human rights Soviet campaigner was Yelena Bonner. A worldwide human rights figure in her own right, she was also the wife of Nobel Peace Prize–winning Soviet atomic physicist Andrei Sakharov, one of his country's leading dissenters and human rights campaigners. Their voices carried tremendous weight, for Sakharov had been a chief developer of the Soviet hydrogen bomb, and knew as well as anyone in the world what risks nuclear weapons brought with them.

Ban-the-bomb groups were also very active in Britain. In 1981, a large group of women campaigners established the Women's Peace Camp at Britain's Greenham Common, at the gates of the U.S. air base at Newbury.

Antiwar Movements

Women were also active in protesting specific wars, most notably by far protesting U.S. participation in the Vietnam War. That issue tore American society apart in the late 1960s and early 1970s, as the war was also supported by massive numbers of Americans. In 1968, pacifist Jeannette

Rankin (see Vol. 8, p. 22) led a march on Washington against the Vietnam War. Rankin had been the only member of the U.S.Congress to have voted against American participation in both world wars.

Another antiwar figure who drew worldwide attention was Guatemalan Rigoberta Menchú (1950–), who was awarded the 1992 Nobel Peace Prize. A Quiché Indian, Menchú had fled her country to Mexico in 1981, after her father and brother had been murdered and her mother raped by government soldiers. There she became one of Latin America's leading peace activists and a spokesperson for many Indian peoples.

Margaret A. Brewer was the first woman to become a brigadier general in the U.S. Marine Corps, in 1978.

Guatemalan peace activist Rigoberta Menchú held a news conference at the United Nations after winning the 1992 Nobel Peace Prize.

The long, bitter civil war in Northern Ireland brought another Nobel Peace Prize, this one awarded in 1976 to Mairead Corrigan, Betty Williams, and Ciaran McKeaun, founders of the Northern Ireland Peace Movement. Their work did not yield peace then, but contributed to more successful efforts in the late 1990s.

Women in the Military

Starting in the mid-1970s, large numbers of women began to enter the U.S. military— though not without continuing problems of discrimination and sexual harassment throughout the male-dominated armed forces. In 1974, the Merchant Marine Academy began admitting women. In 1975, women were by law granted entry to all the service academies, and in 1976, the Military Academy at West Point, the Naval Academy at Annapolis, the Air Force Academy at Colorado Springs, and the Coast Guard Academy all admitted their first women. In 1978, the Women's Armed Forces Integration Act became law, dissolving the separate women's corps and opening all the services to women. Major issues remained, however, most notably

Shannon Faulkner forced The Citadel to admit women, though she herself in the end dropped out of the school.

the admission of women to several other military schools, the still-unsettled issue of women going into combat, and the issue of gay women in the military.

Whether or not women had the right to enter certain other military schools was finally completely settled in 1996, after a highly publicized three-year-long court fight. In 1995, the all-male Citadel military college, in Charleston, South Carolina, had been forced by the federal courts to admit cadet Sharon Faulkner. In 1996, following a U.S. Supreme Court decision, The Citadel

Beverly Gwinn Kelley was the first woman to command a U.S. Coast Guard vessel at sea, in 1979. Two years earlier she had been one of the first women to serve in a military vessel at sea with men.

and Virginia Military Institute gave up their fight and admitted women.

The question of gay women (and men) in the military had not been fully settled in the courts or Congress in the late 1990s, and was still the focus of great and uncertain attention. In 1994, gay U.S. Army colonel

Gail Reals became a brigadier general in the U.S. Marine Corps in 1985, and later was in charge of the Marine base at Quantico, Virginia.

Margarethe Cammermeyer won reinstatement in a widely watched case. As a practical matter, however, gay women in the military seemed to face an uncertain future as the 21st century approached.

On the sexual harassment side, there was no legal uncertainty at all. Sexual discrimination and sexual harassment were clearly illegal, but in fact they were still widely practiced throughout the military, and on all levels.

In one of the most flagrant cases, the Tailhook Scandal, more than 25 women, most of them naval aviators in active service, were sexually attacked by at least 70 male aviators at a 1991 Tailhook naval aviators' association convention in Las Vegas, Nevada. Assaulted helicopter pilot Paula Coughlin brought charges, but her male superiors tried to cover up the scandal and refused to take any action, while Coughlin was forced to resign. After Coughlin went to court, collecting $6.7 million in sexual assault damages, a U.S. secretary of the navy resigned and some senior officers took early retirement—but not one of the male aviators was ever brought to trial.

The 1990s saw many charges of rape and other sexual abuse in the U.S. armed forces, and some convictions as well. By the late 1990s, the army and other services were involved in many investigations, and many indictments were pending, though no one thought that these kinds of problems had yet been solved in the military.

The New Women's Rights Movement

The United States provided fertile soil for the growth of many kinds of political movements during the 1960s and 1970s. A massive civil rights movement was in full swing and growing fast (see "Women in Civil Rights," p. 22). From the mid-1960s, a huge nationwide argument raged about the Vietnam War (see "War and Peace," p. 26). In political life, there were Hippies, Yippies, and the highly political anarchist New Left, and several other kinds of new right, left, and centrist movements. By the late 1960s, there were also similar movements in many other countries, many of them student movements.

Given the temper of the times, it is not surprising that the women's rights movement revived and quickly became a powerful force in American life. Women had never stopped calling for new laws and new attention to be paid to women's rights issues, but the focus had largely been elsewhere during the years of Depression, world war, and postwar rebuilding.

The new wave in women's rights politics came with a rush, triggered by the tremendous response to the publication of a single book: *The Feminine Mystique* (1963) by Betty Friedan (see p. 34). It became the "bible" of the new American women's rights movement. There had been other such works, notably Simone de Beauvoir's *The Second Sex* (see Vol. 9, p. 26). However, Friedan's book struck a mass nerve. It made hundreds of thousands and then millions of women all over the world sit up sharply, take stock of themselves and their situation, and move to change their lives for the better.

Above: *Simone de Beauvoir was still a major feminist figure worldwide. Here she was a guest of Israeli prime minister Levi Eshkok in 1967.*

A key women's rights leader, Gloria Steinem helped shape the movement as the longtime editor of Ms. Magazine, *which she founded in 1969, two years after this picture was taken.*

Another pioneering American feminist of the "new wave" was journalist Gloria Steinem (1934–). In 1963—the same year as Friedan's book—she published the exposé article "I Was a Playboy Bunny," after working in one of the sexist Playboy clubs of the time. Steinem went on to become a leading moderate reformer in the new women's rights movement. As the first and longtime editor of *Ms.* magazine (1971–1989), she helped shape that movement, becoming

one of its chief writers and media celebrities.

Many other leading women's rights movement reformers went on to substantial careers in politics, law, and social reform, and as authors. Among them were Congresswoman and vice-presidential candidate Geraldine Ferraro; Supreme Court Justice Ruth Bader Ginsburg; Congresswoman Bella Abzug; author Elizabeth Janeway; and National Organization for Women (NOW) presidents Eleanor Smeal, Molly Yard, and Patrica Ireland.

Forming the majority of the organized American women's rights movement, the moderates developed substantial political organizations such as the National Women's Political Caucus (NWPC). These

Bella Abzug was a strong campaigner for women's rights and against war, in the U.S. Congress and in such organizations as Women Strike for Peace, which she cofounded.

Betty Friedan

Betty Goldstein Friedan (1921–) had a message very familiar to women of the late 20th century—just as it would have been to women much earlier in the century, though it had been forgotten by some for a time. She urged women to turn away from seeing themselves only as wives and mothers, instead moving out to live full lives in American society as independent people, building their own careers and earning their own incomes. In the world of the late 1990s, with women and men in a large number of families working, that is hardly even advice, but rather economic necessity. In 1963, however, when the "ideal" woman was wholly dependent on the male family breadwinner, her advice was strong stuff. It broke open a whole new outlook for enormous numbers of women.

Friedan's message was the right message at the right time. Within months, women were on the move, with many of them going back to school, finding jobs, meeting together to solve mutual problems, forming their own organizations, and beginning to resist sexual discrimination and harassment—in short, making a lot more of themselves than had before seeemed at all possible.

Soon a political and social movement emerged, a powerful one, for now the energy and attention of millions of women had been caught. Friedan was a founder and first president of the National Organization for Women (NOW) in 1966, leading that increasingly strong organization for the next four years. By 1970, however, she found herself in disagreement with many of its leading members, who were more radical than she, for she was a reformer, not a revolutionary. She did not change her views or full commitment, but continued to press forward on a wide range of women's rights and women's economic freedom matters, as well as urging passage of the Equal Rights Amendment (see p. 38).

Friedan's later works included *The Second Stage* (1981), which was critical of some trends in the radical women's movement. She later also took up the problems faced by older women, in *The Fountain of Age* (1993).

would function as pressure groups on the whole range of women's issues, among them the question of childbearing choice (see "Women's Bodies, Women's Lives," p. 78) and educational and workplace equality (see "Women at Work," p. 47, and "Women in Education," p. 56).

In 1970, the National Organization for Women organized and financed the NOW Legal Defense and Education Fund, to work on pending court cases and other legal matters, and to develop nationwide educational programs and publications on women's issues. Through it, NOW began

Betty Friedan

publishing a large body of widely used publications. There were many similar organizations as well, such as the Women's Legal Defense Fund.

Women of both parties in Congress organized the Congressional Caucus for Women's Issues, to develop information on a wide range of matters affecting women. Several organizations were also established on the purely fund-raising side, such as the Democratic Party women's group Emily's List (1985), which began directly raising and contributing campaign funds to selected candidates for office.

Several new women's groups were organized on an ethnic basis. Among these were the North American Indian Women's Association (1970), National Black Women's Political Leadership Caucus (1971), and National Conference of Puerto Rican Women (1972). These added their presence to a large number of earlier such groups long in existence.

Ti-Grace Atkinson was a radical feminist leader in the late 1960s and early 1970s, her face here superimposed on a "Freedom for Women" button.

Many college-age women became active in the movement against the Vietnam War, like these in the Peace Moratorium offices in 1969.

Radical Women

From the late 1960s, there were sharp divisions in the American women's rights movement. Most of the disagreement was between those who favored reform as the best approach and those who sought revolutionary change. However, some in the women's movement cared less about approach than about emphasis on specific issues, as was the case with the radical lesbian part of the women's rights movement. Yet others felt that the only possible solution to the age-old question of women's freedom lay in the development of new kinds of religious beliefs. These included the spiritual feminists, led by philosopher Mary Daly, and the eco-feminists, linking environmentalism with ideas about earth goddesses.

There were many disagreeing or dissident submovements, some of them quite small, with their organizations sometimes numbering only a few people. But they were also often very committed and very vocal, generating a good deal of controversy within and beyond the women's rights movement.

Some of the most radical leaders of this period had come out of the New Left, the revolutionary, anarchist-leaning part of the mid-1960s movement against the Vietnam War. However, many women found the New Left entirely male-dominated and thoroughly sexist, the kind of movement that once again called on its female members to hold off on women's issues while the men solved the "larger" issues, a very old argument (see "Women's Rights and the Vote," Vol. 6, p. 61).

In the late 1960s and early 1970s, some hundreds of these women gave up on the New Left and formed their own radical feminist groups. Among these were the Radical Women (1967), The Feminists (1968), Redstockings (1969), Women's International Terrorist Conspiracy from Hell (WITCH, 1968), and Radicalesbians (1970). Several well-known radical writers and media celebrities were among them, such as Kate Millett, Ti-Grace Atkinson, Shulamith Firestone, Ellen Willis, Jo Freeman, and Andrea Dworkin.

Dworkin and lawyer Catherine MacKinnon focused especially on the sexual abuse of women. They saw pornography as an

Stopping violence against women was a key issue of this demonstration and of the women's rights movement altogether.

The Equal Rights Amendment

The largest single campaign and the greatest single defeat of the modern American women's rights movement was the proposed Equal Rights Amendment to the U.S. Constitution. It read simply:

Equality of rights under the law shall not be denied or abridged by the United States or by any State on account of sex.

The amendment had been proposed by Alice Paul of the National Woman's Rights Party in 1923 (see "Women in Politics," Vol. 8, p.20). It never even came close to adoption in the decades that followed. In 1967, however, it was taken up by the National Organization for Women (NOW) and was NOW's most important single issue for 15 years, until it was finally defeated.

It came close, passing in the House of Representatives (1971) and the Senate (1972) by large majorities. Within a year, it was ratified by 30 of the 38 states needed. However, opposition then began to build, led by Phyllis Schlafly and other antifeminist groups. They convinced many Americans that the ERA and NOW were "antifamily." The times had changed greatly since 1972, and the same conservative tide that swept Ronald Reagan into the presidency in 1980 was able to defeat the ERA, marking a huge setback for the U.S. women's rights movement.

attack on women's civil rights that should be outlawed, not as free speech to be protected by the First Amendment to the U.S. Constitution. Some radical feminists welcomed such views, going on to organize, to picket, and sometimes even to burn bookstores. Many conservative activists also welcomed such views; they were already trying to outlaw pornography—often while attacking the women's rights movement on a wide range of other issues. The vast majority of women's rights advocates disagreed with Dworkin and MacKinnon, as did the U.S. Supreme Court—but the issue remained still very much alive.

The women's rights movement also found itself opposed by many women.

Most notable of these was antifeminist Phyllis Schlafly, who led the successful fight against adoption of the Equal Rights Amendment (see above), at the head of the Stop ERA and Eagle Forum organizations. Another highly visible opponent was author Camille Paglia, who described herself as a radical feminist while sharply attacking modern feminism and "political correctness."

International Gains and Losses

Women's rights advocates organized most fully in the United States, but movements also grew in many other countries. Very often, however, the paths that women took focused on the wide political issues

The 1985 Nairobi World Conference on Women was attended by delegates from more than 140 nations. These from Iran (left and center) were swathed in the full chador, covering them from head to foot.

facing their countries and the world, rather than on specific "women's issues," reflecting long-held differences in the world women's rights movement (see "Women in Politics," Vol. 8, p. 20).

The United Nations Decade for Women began in 1976 and extended to 1985. The United Nations Development Fund for Women, later called UNIFEM, was established to bring women into decision-making positions at the national and local level, to support women's projects, and to foster economic and social advancement in the world's developing countries. One result of the decade was the nonbinding but influential United Nations Convention on the Elimination of All Forms of Discrimination Against Women (1979). However, the periodic conferences held in later years often focused less on women's rights issues than on more general world political and economic issues.

Still, practical gains were being made around the world. Britain passed the Sex Discrimination Act and the Domestic Violence Act in 1975, the same year that Portugal's new constitution guaranteed sexual equality. France passed a Law of Professional Equality in 1983, followed the next year by Australia's Sex Discrimination Act. Ireland legalized divorce in 1995, the last European country to do so.

In the same period, however, women had substantial losses of rights in some parts of the world, with their rights to dress, work, travel, and live freely sometimes severely restricted. In areas that came under Islamic fundamentalist control, for example, many women were forced once again to shroud themselves from head to foot (see "Changing Styles," p. 66) and some were even cut off from access to health care, for reasons of "modesty," while many continued to be the victims of genital mutilation (see "Women's Bodies, Women's Lives," p. 78).

The United Nations Decade for Women began in 1976 and ended in 1985, at a World Conference held in Nairobi, where the Israeli delegation is shown giving a news conference.

For more information on these aspects of women's lives, see the Political Life sections of other volumes in this set. You can look up specific topics, such as "women's rights" or "revolution," in the Master Index to the set, provided at the end of each volume. See also the bibliography page at the end of each volume.

Illustrated History of Women

Religion, Education, and Everyday Life

Changing Lives

During the late 20th century, women's lives began to change markedly. That was so all over the world, though the pace of change was greatest among women in the relatively rich countries of North America and Europe, and for educated and well-to-do women in many other countries. Their lifestyles and attitudes often reflected Western material wealth and increased freedom, as seen worldwide in Western television and movies. Some of these changes brought major new possibilities of freedom, but they brought problems as well.

Tens of millions of women went to work, more and more freely and often in jobs that had earlier been denied them. Women entered business and the professions in great numbers, fought through many issues of equality in education and in the workplace, including laws against discrimination and sexual harassment (see "Women at Work," p. 47). They also made gains on such matters as maternal leave and other health care issues. Far more than ever before, women were able to build independent lives, incomes, and lifestyles.

The two-working-parent family and the working-single-parent family became common. A never-ending array of gadgets appeared that were supposed to make housekeeping easier and more efficient. Fast-food takeouts tended to replace home cooking, while a wide variety of new child care arrangements grew. On the other hand, some women were focusing on such matters as gourmet cooking and house decorating, guided by women such as Julia Child and Martha Stewart.

Above: *In the late 20th century, market researchers began examining every aspect of women's lives, as here in a mock living room in 1975.*

Women were coming on, but there were also new economic realities. Even in the United States, the world's richest country, the era of the single breadwinner was gone. World populations were growing, world resources shrinking, and there was new competition in all kinds of markets. The world had become a harder place in which to make a living, even in the richer countries, and the rise of women occurred when the economic realities were changing.

Very large numbers of women worked not because they wanted to, but because

Martha Stewart was a notable homemaker's guru in the late 20th century, with advice on everything from pillows to peanuts.

they had to. And they often worked harder than ever before. With all the new labor-saving devices and changing lifestyles, the vast majority of working women actually worked a double shift. They worked, brought in money, built careers—and at the same time had the major responsibility of "taking care" of the home and their families. In short, they were expected to be "superwomen." Some men "helped," but only a very few were full partners.

Poor Women

Such changes, and whatever problems they involved, had little effect on the mass of the world's women. They were to a large

Often with the help of the United Nations, many countries developed educational centers for women. This young woman was learning advanced sewing skills at a center in Libya in 1969.

extent still trapped by poverty, backbreaking and ill-paid work, huge health problems, and social and political conditions in many of the world's completely male-dominated societies.

Poor women in the developing countries—who had child after child and had to walk many miles every day just to get fast-disappearing wood to heat their homes—had little chance to enjoy the benefits of change. For them, change was often for the worse, not for the better.

That was especially so for many of the hundreds of millions of women forced off the land into the cities. In many countries, these immigrants could not even find ill-

In the late 20th century, many families lived in trailers, often with all the modern conveniences.

paid jobs and had to try to take care of their families with very little or nothing in the way of health care, sanitation, clean water, and food.

Changes in Marriage

One massive change in the late 20th century was a rise in the number of couples who lived together without being married, starting in the 1960s. Through the 1970s, many couples experienced legal difficulties if they lived together unmarried. They might lose their jobs, for example, or be barred from certain professions, such as the law. But over the coming decades, these barriers would largely be removed.

Many women still spent their lives on the move, at least seasonally, like this family in Afghanistan in the 1970s.

In previous times, a woman who lived with a man unmarried was regarded as a "loose woman," with a questionable reputation. That would still remain true in much of the world. However, especially in North America and Europe, by the 1990s couples from their teens to their nineties were choosing to live together unmarried. Some did so as a "trial marriage," but others saw no reason to get married, especially if no children were involved.

Another massive change in this period was the rise in the divorce rates. In previous times, divorces were, where allowed, difficult to get. They often involved lengthy and bitter court battles. That would remain so for some couples, who were unable to work out their differences on their own. But the liberalization of divorce laws made ending a marriage far less painful and more common.

With divorce came a whole set of new family patterns. Children often spent part of their time with each parent. New relationships often brought new children, so families very often came to involve stepsiblings and half-siblings.

Divorce also often meant that many older women were left on their own, with little support and few skills. Many widows were left on their own as well, as women lived longer than ever before—and longer than men. A large new population of older women also emerged and began to mobilize to deal with their special problems and concerns.

Traditional Marriage

In much of the world, however, many women still found themselves trapped in traditional patterns of marriage. In many places, including India and some Islamic countries, marriages were still arranged by parents. In some cases, the bride and groom did not even meet until the wedding.

Centuries-old marriage arrangement patterns also continued. In India, for example, a bride's parents were still expected to give the husband's family a dowry (see "Everyday Life of Women in the East and Beyond," Vol. 1, p. 90). Unfortunately, centuries-old abuses also existed. Even in the 1990s, a newly married woman whose family failed to pay promised money or goods as part of a marriage agreement might be abused by her new husband and his family. Some were even killed, in a practice common enough to be termed *dowry murder*.

In many areas, even in the United States, traditional ways continued. This young Amish woman was selling homemade breads and preserves from a stand in Pennsylvania.

The television came to occupy a central place in homes around the world, as here, where an American family was watching then–presidential candidate John F. Kennedy in 1960.

Women in traditional societies also faced other kinds of problems, among them questions of control over their own lives (see "Women's Bodies, Women's Lives," p. 78).

Violence against Women

One pattern that seemed to cut across social and economic boundaries, affecting both rich and poor, was violence against women. Battering, rape, and other abuse of women and children were not new. However, with all the other social changes, the pattern of violence remained.

What was new in the late 20th century was the development of a network of sup-port groups and shelters to provide battered women with a safe haven. In some cases, women's organizations directly founded and ran such shelters. In other cases, they focused their attention on getting government funding for such support networks— and on changing laws and the attitudes of those who enforce the laws.

For the vast majority of women around the world, however, the pattern of violence exists unabated. In some parts of the world, in fact, far worse patterns exist. There young girls may be sold into prostitution or slavery. Though individuals and governments verbally attack such practices, they still continue.

Seeking to improve the lives of children, reformer Marian Wright Edelman founded the Children's Defense Fund in 1973, serving as its longtime president.

Women at Work

Women often work because they must. However, the story of working women in the late 20th century is that of a powerful new drive for historic goals—and of several ideas whose time has come.

In the United States, a major part of that new drive for historic goals began in 1961, when President John F. Kennedy named Eleanor Roosevelt to chair the new President's Commission on the Status of Women. The commission had been proposed by Kennedy's newly appointed head of the Women's Bureau, Esther Peterson (1906–1997). As executive vice-chair of the new commission, she would do most of its day-to-day work.

Esther Peterson, an assistant secretary of labor, was a veteran lobbyist for labor who had worked for the Amalgamated Clothing Workers of America and the AFL-CIO before her appointment. She would later become special assistant to the president for consumer affairs in the administrations of Lyndon B. Johnson and Jimmy Carter. Eleanor Roosevelt was by then the world's leading woman (see Vol. 9, p. 13), who once again set out to make a major contribution.

The commission's work quickly bore fruit. In 1962, President Kennedy began to take steps aimed at guaranteeing equality of opportunity in employment. The following year Congress passed and Kennedy signed the Equal Pay Act, which—despite some weaknesses—was sharply aimed at ending pay discrimination because of sex. Also in 1963, the commission issued its

Above: *Most telephone operators were still women, but they increasingly worked not in front of switchboards but before computer consoles, like this early one.*

In the late 20th century, many women broke into jobs traditionally held by males. Elizabeth Watson was the first woman to head the Houston Police Department.

book is often hailed, and rightly so, as the beginning of a new wave in the American women's movement. At the same time, it played a huge role in a new drive for a set of old, as-yet unfulfilled goals, dealing as it did with the long fight for equal educational and workplace opportunities. For women ready to try to build a new day, the twin impacts of the Roosevelt Commission and the Friedan book were tremendous.

A massive and basic breakthrough came with passage of the Civil Rights Act of 1964, which also set up the Equal Employment Opportunity Commission (EEOC). Title VII

Like many men at the top level, Elizabeth Dole moved back and forth between government and the private sector, as U.S. secretary of transportation, later of labor, and head of the Red Cross.

landmark report *American Women*, which strongly and very effectively urged equality for women in wages, employment opportunities, and educational opportunities, along with special help for working mothers, including maternity leave and partial government funding of day care centers.

In that same year, 1963, Betty Friedan published *The Feminine Mystique*, which urged women to move out into the wider world, building their own careers and living independent lives (see p. 34). Friedan's

Construction jobs were always hard for women to get, except in family businesses, but women made some breakthroughs in the late 20th century.

of the act banned employment discrimination because of sex, race, color, religion, or national origin, legally opening the way to many changes that would follow during the rest of the century.

In the workplace, the long fight for equal rights and opportunities continued, for commissions, books, new laws, enforcement agencies, court cases, and organizations could not quickly change long-established and worldwide patterns of discrimination against working

women. In the United States, for example, there were far more women in business and the professions in the mid-1990s than there had been in the mid-1960s—but the overwheming majority of top business and financial executives were still men, as was so in such professions as law, medicine, and the sciences.

The situation was so bad that the term "glass ceiling" came into general use, meaning an invisible but very real barrier through which very few women could pass.

Many young women were able to move into management positions through franchising, like this Chinese-American woman running a fast-food restaurant.

It remained that way. In 1995, the U.S. Glass Ceiling Commission, established by Congress, reported that women and minority group members were still very rarely found in top management. The same basic situation was widely observed in the kinds of professions traditionally dominated by men.

Another term that came into general use was the "mommy track." That was the of-ten-denied but very real practice of placing women who chose to work and also to have children on a much slower promotion track than women who chose to focus solely on their careers.

By the mid-1990s, more than half of all adult U.S. women worked for pay outside their homes—but the great majority were working because they needed the money, and at jobs paying far less than those occupied mostly by men. Most were working in "traditional" women's jobs, as clerical workers, waitresses, domestic workers, low-ranked hospital employees, retail and other service workers, and semiskilled farm and factory workers.

Many women office workers spent much of their day on the telephone, like this bill collector.

Women also began to move into banking jobs, as tellers and increasingly as managers at the branch level and higher.

For single mothers, the job situation had also changed very much for the worse. Far more women than ever before were attempting to support their families alone, because divorce and desertion rates had skyrocketed from the 1960s on. Women heading single-parent families often had very little in the way of skills and worked at low-paid, hard jobs, while also working full-time as single parents. They often received little or no support from the fathers of their children, had very little time or money for education, and were effectively trapped in poverty and exhaustion. Those who were members of minority groups had all the problems of single mothers, magnified by their even greater difficulty in getting and holding any jobs at all. Some people were highly critical of "welfare mothers," and federal, state, and local wel-

fare rules were tightened, making the lives of such women even harder—although study after study made it clear that most poor women infinitely preferred to learn, work, and earn their own way in the world, if given half a chance.

Even so, the long battle for equality continued, and there were some real gains. In 1973, the American Telephone & Telegraph Company (AT&T), an enormous nationwide employer, signed a federal consent decree promising to end some major sex discrimination policies throughout the company.

In 1978, a major breakthrough for pregnant women came with passage of the U.S. Pregnancy Discrimination Act. This banned discrimination because of pregnancy, childbirth, or related conditions in businesses employing 15 or more people.

Anita Faye Hill and Clarence Thomas

The outstanding sexual harassment case of the late 20th century involved the charges brought by law professor Anita Faye Hill (1956–) against Judge Clarence Thomas—both politically conservative African-Americans.

In July 1991, President George Bush nominated Thomas to the U.S. Supreme Court. During the normal FBI investigation of Thomas, Hill charged Thomas with having sexually harassed her while she was his assistant at the Education Department's Office of Civil Rights and then at the Equal Employment Opportunity Commission. The Judiciary Committee, deadlocked, sent Thomas's nomination to the full Senate without mentioning Hill's charges. Just before the Senate vote on the Thomas nomination, news and broadcast media began reporting Hill's accusations. Hill then "went public" with her charges. A firestorm erupted and the committee was forced to reopen hearings, which were then conducted before a worldwide television audience (October 11–13).

The extraordinary hearings were also extraordinarily bitter, with some Republican senators even publicly charging Hill with perjury, while Thomas denied all charges and accused his opponents of racism. Ultimately, Thomas was confirmed by a Republican Senate and became a Supreme Court justice, though one whose personal reputation was damaged. Hill lost her battle and emerged as a controversial figure—but a heroine to the worldwide women's movement. Though her treatment might have stopped others from filing sexual harassment charges, in fact the opposite happened, for the number of such filings increased in the next few years. The case was also thought to have energized the women's movement and greatly contributed to the election victories of many women candidates in the 1992 U.S. elections.

Anita Hill

Sexual Harassment

One of the chief battlegrounds in the fight for women's equality in the workplace was in the area of sexual harassment, which continued to be defined and redefined by law and in the courts throughout the final decades of the century. The issue was taken up most forcefully in the United States. One outstanding sexual harassment case was that involving Anita Faye Hill (see p. 52). Another involved sexual harassment charges made by at least 17 women against Oregon senator Bob Packwood in the early 1990s. In 1995, after the Senate Ethics Committee recommended his expulsion, Packwood resigned.

In 1993, Justice Sandra Day O'Connor, speaking for a unanimous U.S. Supreme Court, wrote the landmark *Harris v. Forklift Systems* decision, making it far easier for women in the workplace to prove sexual harassment. Even so, sexual harassment continued to be a major problem in some areas, most notably the military (see "War and Peace," p. 26).

The issue became international, as well. In 1994, the United Nations agreed to pay damages to women employees charging sexual harassment. New sexual discrimination laws in Britain, Canada, New Zealand, and Australia also made it possible for women to bring charges of sexual harassment.

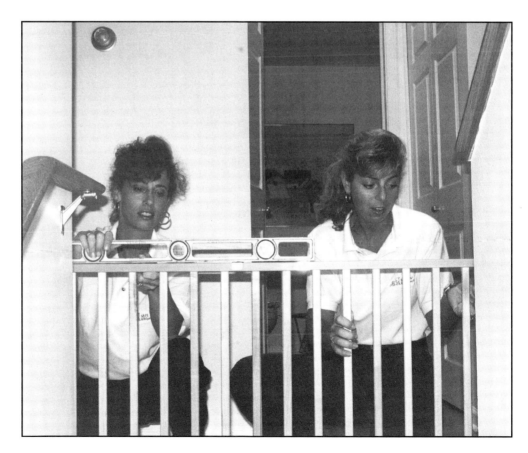

As always, many women founded their own businesses, like these two partners who founded Chicago's Safe 'n' Sound Childproofers.

Women in the News

As the whole world of work began to change for women in the 1960s and 1970s, so did the world of journalism. Although the newspaper industry was still largely male-dominated, far more women began to work in regular news reporting jobs on major newspapers, rather then being confined in the ghetto of the "woman's page."

One was Lucinda Franks, who in 1971 became the first woman and the youngest person to win a Pulitzer Prize for national reporting, shared with Thomas Powers. A second was Helen Thomas (1920–), who in 1974 became the first woman to head the White House bureau of a major news service (United Press International). A year later she was elected the first woman president of the White House Correspondents Association. A third was Mary McGrory, who in 1975 was the first woman to win a Pulitzer Prize for commentary. Women would receive scores of Pulitzers in the years and decades that followed.

On the publishing side, Katherine Graham (1917–) took over the operation of the *Washington Post* after the suicide of her husband, Philip Graham, in 1963. In the years that followed, and especially during the Watergate scandal, she emerged as a leading publisher, who built the *Post* into one of the world's great newspapers.

Women Broadcasters

Broadcast journalism brought new female celebrities, for the 1960s and 1970s saw the beginning of a major breakthrough

Above: *Katherine Graham, shown here in 1976, was publisher of the* Washington Post *from 1963, making it a major international newspaper.*

Noted as an interviewer since her days on the "Today" show in the 1960s, Barbara Walters was the first woman to be an anchor on a major network's evening news show, at ABC (1976–1978).

for women in television. One of the earliest of the top women in television was Barbara Walters (1931–). She worked as a writer in television in the 1950s and early 1960s, before breaking into broadcasting on the "Today" show in 1963. She was a regular panelist on that show until 1974, and then cohosted the show with Hugh Downs until 1976. Walters made a breakthrough as the first woman evening news anchor for a major network (1976–1978), coanchoring the "ABC Evening News" with Harry Reasoner. She remained one of television's leading interviewers, in her long series of "Barbara Walters Specials" (1976–) and on "20/20" (1979–).

The second woman and first Asian-American to coanchor a major network's evening news show was Connie Chung (1946–), who coanchored the "CBS Evening News" with Dan Rather (1993–1996). Another pioneer newscaster was Pat Harper (1935–1994), who in 1980 became the first woman to anchor a nationally syndicated evening news show, coanchored with her husband, Joe Harper. She and Chuck Scarborough later coanchored New York's Emmy-winning WNBC-TV evening news show.

Connie Chung began her career in local television in Washington, D.C., later coanchoring the "CBS Evening News" (1993–1996).

Women in Education

In the United States, major changes began to rock the male-dominated college and university world in the 1960s, and continued during the rest of the century. To some extent, those changes began to come in 1963, with the fast growth of the new women's movement, helped greatly by the work of Eleanor Roosevelt's presidential commission, which demanded equality of opportunity in education (see "Women at Work," p. 47).

The first visible sign that a new day had begun was the explosive growth of women's studies. The first women's studies program was established at San Diego State College in 1969. Within a few years there were hundreds and then thousands of such programs in operation.

The truly massive breakthrough, however, came in 1972, with the passage of Title IX of the 1972 Education Act Amendments. This banned discrimination in most feder-ally assisted educational programs and activities, including sports (see "Women in Sports," p. 70). In 1988, after a Supreme Court ruling had muddied the antidiscrimination waters, Congress passed a law making it clear that Title IX applied to all higher education programs, whether federally funded or not.

Educational discrimination was under attack in several countries. Britain's 1975 Sexual Discrimination Act was weak in many areas, but did force the opening of the Rhodes Scholarships to women. In the later 1980s and in the 1990s, several other countries banned sexual discrimination in education, among them Canada, Australia, and New Zealand.

Above: *In the late 20th century, many United States schools established bilingual educational programs. This young Chinese-American was showing off her calligraphy.*

Even before Title IX, the walls were beginning to come down, as women undergraduates were admitted for the first time to such major universities as Yale (1969), Princeton (1970), and scores of other colleges and universities. Several formerly all-women colleges and universities also began to admit male students.

More women began to teach on college faculties as well, but much discrimination persisted in higher faculty positions, and continued into the late 1990s. In one very notable incident, Derrick Bell, the first African-American professor at Harvard Law School, resigned after unsuccessfully campaigning for the school to hire and give tenure to what would have been its first African-American woman tenured professor.

Alice Rivlin was a professor at George Mason University and a staff member at the Brookings Institution before joining President Bill Clinton's Office of Management and Budget.

Hanna Holborn Gray was the first woman to become president of a top American coeducational university, the University of Chicago, in 1978.

There were also still strong barriers to women in college administration, as the vast majority of college presidents continued to be men. There was movement, though. In 1975, Australian-born Jill Ker Conway (1934–) became the first woman president of Smith College. Three years later, Hanna Holborn Gray (1930–) became the first woman president of a top American coeducational university, the University of Chicago. There were others, as well, and not only in the United States. In 1976, Hélène Ahrweiler (1967–) became the first woman president of the Sorbonne and was later named chancellor of the Universities of Paris (1982). In 1983, Chinese physicist Xie Xide (1921–) became president of Fudan

In the United States, small schoolhouses like this one gave way to large central schools in the late 20th century, though rural schoolhouses were still common in many other parts of the world.

University. Another trailblazer was Marguerite Ross Barnett (1942–1992), who in 1990 became the first woman and the first African-American president of the University of Houston.

Women also moved more freely between high university positions and government, as men had been doing for a long time. One outstanding example was that of Donna Shalala (1941–), who was the president of Hunter College (1980–1988), president of the University of Wisconsin (1988–1992), and then U.S. secretary of health and and human services (1993–). Another was U.S. budget director Alice Rivlin (1931–), a former university professor and a past

president of the American Economic Association. A third very notable example was that of Madeleine Albright (1937–), who went from her job as a professor at Georgetown University's School of Foreign Service to the post of U.S. ambassador to the United Nations, and then to that of U.S. secretary of state, the first woman in the post (see "Women, Power, and Politics, " p. 10).

Donna Shalala headed Hunter College, then the University of Wisconsin, before going on to become the U.S. secretary of health and human services.

Women in Religion

Women in religion continued to play what had become their traditional roles during the late 20th century. At the same time, they developed a much more intense fight for equality.

Playing traditional roles often meant caring for the poor and ill, and contributing to general and religious education. Mother Teresa (see "Women in Education and Religion," Vol. 9, p. 66), founder and head of the worldwide Catholic Missionaries of Charity order, continued to be one of the world's leading religious figures. She was awarded the 1979 Nobel Peace Prize.

A second major figure was Australian Salvation Army leader Eva Burrows (1930–). In 1986 she became international chief commander of the Army, its first woman international head since Evangeline Booth (see "Women in Religion," Vol. 8, p. 59).

Many women dedicated their lives to their religions, as earlier often working with religious organizations to help those who were poor and in need of medical care all over the world. As had always been so, many did their work at risk of their own lives and health. In one tragic instance, in 1980, four Maryknoll nuns working in El Salvador were murdered by right-wing death squads during that country's civil war. Other women (and men) working in relief organizations were also killed or injured in combat zones, as happened in sub-Saharan Africa again and again during the many disastrous wars of the late 20th century. Many were also stricken with

Above: *In 1989 Barbara Clementine Harris became the first woman bishop of the Episcopal Church and of the Anglican Communion worldwide.*

Sally Preisand became the first woman rabbi in Reform Judaism when she was ordained in Cincinnati, Ohio, in 1972.

physical feminists, such as Robin Morgan, attempted to build new religions based on "goddess worship" and other substitutes for major religions they saw as the "patriarchal"—that is, entirely male-dominated. These beliefs were sometimes linked to theories about presumed early "mother goddesses" (see "Venus Figurines and Mother Goddesses," Vol. 1, p. 14).

Women's status in religions had been debated for more than a century (see "Women in Religion," Vol. 7, p. 46). As the drive for equality grew in the late 20th century, the debate became far more widespread and intense. Some breakthroughs then began to come, especially on the hotly

The Missionaries of Charity was just one of many orders dedicated to helping the poor and the sick. Here Mother Teresa prepared to leave for a region devastated by a cyclone in 1977.

infectious diseases, as happened during the massive worldwide AIDS epidemic of the 1980s and 1990s.

Women's Status in Religion

Late in the 20th century, the status of women emerged as a major set of issues in several of the world's great religions. Beyond that, some women questioned the religions themselves, feeling that women's second-class status in their religions could never be solved. Some thought the solution lay in building new religions. Spiritual feminists, such as Mary Daly, and meta-

Many strongly religious people opposed abortion absolutely, like this woman, while others supported a woman's right to an abortion.

argued issue of women becoming ministers or rabbis. In 1965, for example, Rachel Henderlite became the first ordained Presbyterian minister in the United States. Seven years later, in 1972, fulfilling a promise made half a century earlier (see "Women in Religion," Vol 8, p. 59), Sally Preisand be-

came the first American woman to be ordained a rabbi of Reform Judaism, while Barbara Cantor became its first woman cantor in 1975. Ten years after that, in 1985, Amy Eilberg was the first American woman to become a Conservative rabbi.

The worldwide Anglican Communion—which includes several national Episcopal and Anglican churches, among them the Church of England—played an especially notable role in the ordination of women. In 1977, Mary Michael Simpson became the first Episcopal nun to win ordination as a priest in the United States. She was followed by many others. Among them was African-American Episcopal priest Barbara Clementine Harris, who in 1989 was the first woman to become a bishop of the Episcopal Church and of the worldwide Anglican Communion.

In 1992, after a long, often-bitter fight, the English and Australian Anglican churches decided to accept the ordination of women. In 1994, the first 32 British women Anglican priests were ordained, in a mass ceremony at Bristol Cathedral.

The worldwide Catholic Church, on the other hand, refused to ordain women priests, despite a powerful movement within that church, most notably in the United States. Some small concessions were made toward women. However, even into the late 1990s, the Catholic Church held on to existing bars against women as priests and strongly resisted the movement toward the equality of women within the church. As a result, many nuns and women educators left the church, while others stayed only very uncertainly.

Flying High

In the late 20th century, humanity flew very high indeed. High into the atmosphere, and higher still, out to the stars, for the age of space flight had come.

On April 12, 1961, Soviet flier Yuri Gagarin became the first astronaut in space, circling the earth once in the spacecraft *Vostok 1*. A few weeks later on May 5, U.S. astronaut Alan Shepard followed him into space, on the spacecraft *Freedom 7*.

The first woman in space was Soviet astronaut Valentina Tereshkova (1937–), who on June 16, 1963, began orbiting the earth in the Soviet spacecraft *Vostok 6*. That voyage would see her circle the Earth 48 times in 71 hours, covering 1.2 million miles. Tereshkova was heaped with honors on her

Above: *American astronaut Shannon Lucid set a new women's record for a stay in space, after 188 days in the Soviet space station* Mir *in 1996.*

Soviet cosmonaut Valentina Tereshkova was the first woman in space, circling the earth 48 times in the spacecraft Vostok 6 *in 1963.*

Astronaut Sally Ride was the first American woman in space, as flight engineer on Space Shuttle 7 *in 1983.*

return and remained a Soviet and Russian hero for decades. Many Russian women followed her into space, among them Elena Kondakova, who spent a then-record 169 days in space aboard the Russian space station *Mir* (1994–1995).

Twenty years after Tereshkova's first voyage, U.S. astronaut Sally Ride (1951–) became the first American woman in space, as flight engineer on *Space Shuttle 7*, in 1983.

American women in space hit the news in an entirely different way in 1986. On January 28, the U.S. space shuttle *Challenger* exploded only a minute after its liftoff from Cape Canaveral, Florida. All seven people aboard died immediately, including astro-

naut Judith A. Resnick and an observer, teacher (Sharon) Christa McAuliffe. An elementary error had been made; a key, very small elastic part (an O-ring) had become predictably inelastic when it became ice-cold in the winter weather.

In 1996, U.S. astronaut Shannon Wells Lucid (1943–) set a new women's record of 188 days in space aboard the Russian space staton *Mir*, breaking Elena Kondakova's record. That was also the most time any American had spent in space. Lucid was voted a Congressional Space Medal of Honor.

Teacher Christa McAuliffe, shown here trying on her space suit, and Judith Resnick were two of the seven people who lost their lives in 1986, when space shuttle Challenger *exploded in midair.*

Donna Shirley headed NASA's Mars exploration project and was chief developer of the 1996–1997 series of American Mars probes, including the exploration robot vehicle Sojourner, *shown with her.*

Another notable woman in the American space program was Dr. Donna S. Shirley. As head of the Mars exploration project at the National Aeronautics and Space Administration's Space Jet Propulsion Laboratory, she was the chief developer of the 1996–1997 series of American Mars probes, including the exploration robot vehicle *Sojourner*.

Women in the Air

Women also continued to play a role in

piloted aircraft during this period. Many were flight attendants (formerly called *stewardesses*) and increasing numbers were pilots. Many others continued to be active on the manufacturing side, most notably Olive Beech (see "Women in the Air," Vol. 9, p. 55).

In addition, women continued to score some "firsts" in air flight. One very notable flier was British aviator Sheila Scott (1927–1988). In 1965 she made the longest-ever solo flight around the world, flying 31,000 miles in 189 hours in air. In 1971, Scott was

British aviator Sheila Scott made the first solo light-aircraft flight around the world via the North Pole, in 1971.

Many women worked in the air as flight attendants. They were previously called stewardesses *and were originally all nurses, for safety reasons.*

the first to fly solo around the world from equator to equator, over the North Pole.

A second extraordinary feat was that of aviators Jeana Yeager and Dick Rutan. In 1985 they flew nonstop around the world in their aircraft *Voyager*, designed to be so small and so light that Yeager and Rutan were able to complete the flight without refueling.

A third quite unusual aviator was U.S. flier Marion Rice Hart (1892–1990), who in 1966, at the age of 74, made the first of her six solo flights across the Atlantic. She had decades earlier sailed around the world with a crew of four (1936–1939).

Vicki Van Meter was the youngest girl to fly across the United States, at age 11 in 1993. She handled the flight completely on her own, though she was accompanied by her instructor, as required by law for flyers under the age of 16. The next year she became the youngest woman to fly across the Atlantic Ocean.

On a far sadder note, the desire to be "first" can also lead to tragedy, as it did in 1996 for seven-year-old Jessica Dubroff. She, her father, and her flight instructor died during a takeoff in a rainstorm, while she was trying to become the youngest person ever to fly across North America from coast to coast.

Changing Styles

Fashion patterns that had ruled women for generations seemed to disappear in the late 20th century, starting in the 1960s. Hats and gloves, which had been essential for the well-dressed woman, largely disappeared. Hats would not begin to make a comeback until the late 1990s.

Carefully permed and lacquered hairdos gave way to more natural styles. Long, straight hair was common in the 1960s, with shorter, casual styles coming in during the 1970s. The 1980s brought a wide variety of styles, including colors such as green and blue and hair chopped or pulled into spikes, while the 1990s was dominated by the "big hair" look.

The miniskirt, introduced in the 1960s by British designer Mary Quant (1934–), was

Above: *A blouse and pinafore were a popular outfit for young girls, like this one playing school.*

Big shirts and big hair were the fashion in the 1990s, as here worn by country singer Reba McEntire.

When miniskirts were introduced in the 1960s, hats were still in fashion, as worn by this model in 1967.

a radical break with the past. The same period saw the wide popularity of the bikini bathing suit. But the late 1960s and early 1970s also saw the revival of long, traditional-style skirts and blouses. British designer Laura Ashley (1925–1985) was especially known for her clothes derived from 18th- and 19th-century fabric designs. This was at first most popular among women in the "hippie" movement, but would remain an enduring casual style for women to the end of the century.

As women increasingly moved into the workforce, pantsuits became enormously popular. At first, however, they were not widely accepted, as many organizations had official or unofficial "dresses or skirts only" policies for women employees. The same held true of schools, but by late in the century, pants, blue jeans, and even shorts were commonly worn by students. In the 1980s, heavily tailored skirt-suits, called *power suits*, were popular among professional women.

Starting in the 1960s, many women freed themselves from the constrictions of girdles and corsets. Many also threw away their bras, especially feminists who believed that wearing such garments stressed women's physical appearance, causing them to be seen as sexual objects. The lack of constriction also fitted the hippie lifestyle. Most women, however, continued to wear bras, though sometimes in a more natural style. By late in the century, girdles, corsets, and all-in-one foundation garments were mak-

The bikini bathing suit, modeled here in 1968, was a far cry from the blouse, bloomers, and woolen stockings worn at the beginning of the century.

Western styles and ways were adopted widely in Japan in the late 20th century. This is Crown Princess Masako, a professional woman before her marriage, in a suit-dress.

ing a comeback, by then sometimes going under the general name of *shapewear*.

With the late-20th-century popularity of Western culture, especially the movies and television, Western styles also spread around the world. On the other hand, Western designers also drew on traditional styles in their own creations. So, for example, the long, slim dress common in China and the loose gathered trousers worn for centuries in Central Asia influenced the Western slim evening gown styles of the 1970s. Also inspired by traditional styles were the nose-rings, eyebrow-rings, and other body rings

that became fashionable jewelry in the 1990s.

With the rise of Islamic fundamentalism in some countries, however, this trend was sharply reversed. In countries such as Iran in the 1980s and Afghanistan in the 1990s, women had the clock turned back. They were forced to give up Western styles and shroud themselves in the completely enveloping clothing dictated by Islamic rulers. This clothing, which went under various names, including *chador* and *burqa*, completely covered the woman from head to foot, leaving only the face—sometimes only the eyes—exposed.

Another problem related to fashion was

The neat, trim suit was a standard among women in many professions, like University of Tennessee women's basketball coach Pat Summitt.

This Saudi family is having a day at the beach, but the woman is required to remain totally covered except for her eyes. The view of her ankles and underdress are rare, for the same reasons.

the dominance of ultra-thin models, which fostered unrealistic body images for many young women. This helped to create a Western passion for dieting and contributed to a sharp rise in anorexia nervosa, a disease in which women (and some men) starve themselves—sometimes to death. It was a sad social commentary, when so many people around the world were truly starving for lack of food.

Some of the concern over body images focused on the Barbie doll. Developed by Ruth Handler in 1959 and sold by her Mattel toy company, Barbie became one of the most popular toys of the century. However, the waist of these dolls was impossibly thin, compared to the breasts and hips. Many were concerned that they gave young girls distorted ideas about what their bodies should look like as they matured.

The Chinese fashion of a long slim dress, with a slit up the leg for walking, was picked up by Western fashion designers.

Women in Sports

With the coming of television, sports became enormously popular throughout the world. Now it was possible for millions and tens of millions of people to see sports events as they happened. Ultimately, events such as the Olympics would draw audiences of more than a billion people, making the athletes participating in such events into major international celebrities.

Television broadcasting also made it possible for sports—including many women's sports that had not been widely popular—to build large, devoted audiences. All this came at a time when women were pushing ahead toward equality and independence, from the 1960s on. The net result was a worldwide surge in which women athletes broke down barriers throughout the whole range of world sports on every level, from elementary school right up to the creation of brand-new national and worldwide stars.

In the United States, the women's sports situation changed vastly for another related reason as well. With the push toward justice for women and minorities came new civil rights legislation. In sports, that came most notably in the form of Title IX of the 1972 Education Act Amendments, which banned discrimination in most federally assisted educational programs and activities, including sports (see "Women in Education," p. 56). The new law meant that previously starved women's sports programs at all educational levels had to be supplied with money, coaching, playing space, equipment, and all the other

Above: *Six members of the 1996 Olympic-gold-medal-winning U.S. women's gymnastics team posed—(from left) Dominique Moceanu, Shannon Miller, Jaycie Phelps, Amy Chow, Dominique Dawes, and Amanda Borden. Missing was Kerri Strug.*

things that boys' and men's sports had enjoyed all along. Women's athletics then boomed, as women pushed hard and won funds and support. Large numbers of girls and women entered women's athletic programs, and huge new audiences were created for women's college and professional sports events.

Beyond that, women kept posting "firsts." A different kind of "first" came in 1972, when the University of Chicago offered the first U.S. women's athletic scholarships. Two years after that, in 1974, one

In 1996 German runner Uta Pippig was the first to lead the women's field at the Boston Marathon three times in a row—officially. Two others had done so before women were "allowed" to compete.

One of the best women's basketball players ever, Cheryl Miller played before women's professional leagues existed. She later coached a team in the Women's National Basketball Association.

of the most popular "firsts" in the history of U.S. women's sports came, when Little League baseball was opened to girls.

There was certainly still discrimination against women in sports, and in many countries. At the same time, the world of women's sports greatly changed, and for the better. Now women moved into previously mostly male sports, as sailors, jock-

women's sports and in U.S. sports. At the 1964 Tokyo Olympics, Iolanda Balas (1936–) became the first person to win two gold medals in the high jump (1960; 1964).

Four years later, at the 1968 Mexico City Olympics, Czech gymnast Vera Caslavska (1942–) won four gold and two silver medals, even though she had been forced to train while hiding from the Soviet troops who had invaded her country. She would be followed by Soviet gymnast Olga Korbut, the popular star of the 1972 Munich Olympics, who won three gold medals and was the first woman to do a backflip on the balance beam.

These are the Tennessee Tigerbells—(from left) Wilma Rudolph, Lucinda Williams, Barbara Jones, and Martha Hudson—after setting a world record in the women's 400-meter relay at the 1960 Rome Olympics.

eys, boxers, drag racers, dog-sled racers, bullfighters, and much more. Now great new stars and whole new leagues emerged in some sports more closely linked with women, among them figure skating, tennis, golf, track and field, gymnastics, and women's basketball.

New Stars

From the 1960s on, a lot of new stars began to come out, many of them first shining at the Olympics. At the 1960 Rome Olympics, African-American runner Wilma Rudolph (1940–1994) became the first woman to win three gold medals, in the 100 meters, the 200 meters, and the 400-meter relay, making history in worldwide

The most decorated American gymnast ever, Shannon Miller led the women's gymnastics team to its first Olympic medal at the 1996 Atlanta Olympics.

Americans Jenni Meno and Todd Sand won numerous national and international titles in pairs figure skating.

In track and field, a legendary figure was Jackie (Jacqueline) Joyner-Kersee (1962–), one of the world's greatest athletes. Joyner-Kersee won two consecutive Olympic gold medals in the heptathlon (1988; 1992), setting a world record with 7,291 points in 1988. Many runners also became major stars, such as Florence Griffith-Joyner, Gail Devers, Marie-José Pérec, and Mary Decker Slaney.

Figure skating also became a hugely popular sport in this period, helped a great deal by television, which took the high artistry and accompanying music of the skaters right into the world's living rooms. One of the greatest pairs skaters in the history of the sport was Soviet figure skater Lyudmila Yevgenevna Belousova Protopopov (1935–). She and her husband, Oleg Protopopov, won two Olympic gold medals, four world championships, and four European championships, starting in the early 1960s. Another Soviet standout was Irina Rodnina, who won the first of 10 successive world pairs figure skating titles in 1969, with two different partners, Alexei Ulanov (1969–1972) and Aleksander Zaitsev (1973–1978). From Britain came the extraordinary ice-dancing team of Jayne Torvill and Christopher Dean, who won three successive world ice-dancing championships (1981–1983) and revolutionized ice dancing.

Among the women's figure-skating

Ice dancing became widely popular from the early 1980's. These are American ice-dancers Elizabeth Punsalan and Jerod Swallow.

Chen Lu was the first Chinese figure skater ever to win a world singles championship, in 1995.

At the age of 14, Tara Lipinski became the youngest world women's figure skating champion ever, in 1997, capping that with an Olympic gold medal in 1998.

singles standouts were three-time world champion Peggy Fleming (1966–1968), who also won at the 1968 Olympics; four-time world champion Katarina Witt (1984–1985, 1987–1988), who also won at the 1984 and 1988 Olympics; and two-time world champion Kristi Yamaguchi (1991–1992), who also won at the 1992 Olympics. More recent stars included 1995 world champion Chen Lu, China's first figure skating world

champion; 1996 world champion Michelle Kwan, known for her grace and artistry; and Tara Lipinski, the 1997 world and 1998 Olympic figure skating champion, the youngest ever.

Women's basketball became widely popular at the college level. In 1969, Penny Ann Early became the first woman to play professional basketball, in one game with the Kentucky Colonels of the American Basketball Association. However, at that time, women had no "leagues of their own" to play in. Basketball great Nancy Lieberman-Cline later played on the otherwise all-male Springfield Fame in the U.S.

A college basketball star in the late 1970s, Nancy Lieberman-Cline was still playing in her 40s, when she joined the Women's National Basketball Association in 1997.

Basketball League (1986–1987). Early women's professional leagues did not flourish in North America, and many American women went abroad to Europe and Asia, where women's leagues did exist. Then in 1996, the Olympic gold medal–winning U.S. women's basketball team helped spark the formation of *two* successful U.S. women's professional basketball leagues: the American Basketball League (ABL) and the Women's National Basketball Association (WNBA). These provided a showcase and a place to play for hundreds of women basketball stars.

Women champions emerged in several major sports. In 1974, tennis great Chris Evert (1954–) won the first two of her 18 Grand Slam titles, with wins at Wimbledon and the U.S. Open. In 1975, Czech national women's tennis champion Martina Navratilova (1956–) fled to the West. She would become the world's greatest women's tennis player, top-ranked from 1982 to 1985, with a career total of 332 weeks as the world's top woman player, including 271 weeks in a row (a record for women or men). Later great stars included Steffi Graf (1969–), who stayed at the top of women's tennis most of the time from 1987 through the mid-1990s, and Monica Seles (1974–), second only to Graf during the early 1990s.

Golf also produced some notable women stars. Nancy Lopez (1955–) stormed onto the scene in 1978 with nine wins, five of them in a row, both still-standing records. Four-time Ladies' Professional Golf Association Player of the Year, she was still winning tournaments in the 1990s. A top woman golfer of the late 1980s was Betsy King (1955–), twice Player of the Year (1984;

In the early 1980s, tennis star Martina Navratilova spent 271 straight weeks ranked as number one in the world—a record for women or men.

1990). More recent standouts included the Swedish star Annika Sörenstam (1970–), who went from Rookie of the Year in 1994 to Player of the Year in 1995, and Karrie Webb (1974–) who in 1996 was Rookie of the Year and also the LPGA's leading money winner, the first LPGA player to top $1 million in earnings during a single season.

In 1968, U.S. jockey Kathy Kusner became the first American woman to win a license to race horses at major racetracks. A year later, in 1970, Diane Crump was the first woman to ride in the Kentucky Derby. In 1993, Julie Krone would become the first woman jockey to win one of racing's famed

Janet Guthrie looked over the course of the Indianapolis 500 automobile race in 1976. The next year she would become the first woman to compete in the noted race.

who in an earlier day would have been called adventurers, but who now were recognized as major figures in women's sports. One was Japanese mountain-climber Junko Tabei, in 1975 the first woman to reach the top of Mount Everest, as part of an all-woman Japanese team. Another was sailor Sharon Sites Adams, who in 1969 was the first woman to sail alone across the Pacific. Polish sailor Krystyna Chojnowska-Liskiewicz was the first woman to sail alone around the world, in 1976.

"Triple Crown" events, the Belmont Stakes.

A quite major "first" came in 1977, when Janet Guthrie became the first woman to drive in what had been a great fortress of male domination, the Indianapolis 500 automobile race. In that same year, Shirley Muldowney was the first woman to win the National Hot Rod Association's Winston World Championship in drag racing. She would win it twice more (1980; 1981), becoming the first person to win it three times. In racing of a different sort, U.S. dog-sled racer Susan Butcher (1955–) was a four-time winner of Alaska's Anchorage–Nome Iditarod Dog Sled Race.

Finally, there were some women athletes

Japanese mountaineer Junko Tabei celebrated her safe return after becoming the first woman to reach the top of Mt. Everest, in 1975.

For more information on these aspects of women's lives, see the Religion, Education, and Everyday Life sections of other volumes in this set. You can also look up specific topics, such as "education" or "religion," in the Master Index to the set, at the end of each volume. See also the bibliography page at the end of each volume.

Science, Technology, and Medicine

Women's Bodies, Women's Lives

Social, political, and medical changes took place in the late 20th century that had profound effects on women's health and welfare. In many cases, women's bodies became a battleground, with the underlying question being: Who makes decisions relating to a woman's body?

Birth Control and Sex Education

A whole set of massive changes resulted from the introduction of "The Pill" in 1960. Developed by Gregory Pincus, with funds from the Planned Parenthood Federation and American philanthropist Katharine Dexter McCormick, this was the first oral contraceptive—that is, a pill that could prevent pregnancy. It was also far more reliable than any of the previous "barrier" forms of contraception.

The changes that took place in the 1960s and beyond were far wider and deeper than a pill. However, the Pill certainly did play a role in the sexual revolution of that period. Women were now able to prevent pregnancy by choice, with a high degree of effectiveness. That meant women had far more freedom to decide when and with whom to have sex.

Ironically, however, questions of birth control and sex education continued to be a major battleground (see "Birth Control and Sex Education," Vol. 8, p. 85). Not until 1965, in *Griswold v. Connecticut*, did the U.S. Supreme Court uphold the right of married couples to use contraceptives.

While sexual restrictions were being loosened, many women still did not have

Above: *Remembering the many women who died having illegal abortions, the people attending this 1993 Washington rally were concerned that abortion might once again become illegal.*

access to sex education and birth control. Many schools in the United States did come to include sex education programs for their students, and some even came to provide birth control devices. However, these continued to be enormously controversial subjects for public officials.

In a related development, abortion also came to be legalized in many countries (see *"Roe v. Wade,"* p. 82). Many researchers sought a pill that could be used to end a possible pregnancy after conception. RU 486—the so-called abortion pill—was developed in France in 1988, and was widely used in many European countries. Reli-

Janet Grame Travell was the first woman to serve as personal physician to the president (1961–1965), appointed by President John F. Kennedy.

As U.S. surgeon general, Joycelyn Elders championed sex education and availability of contraceptives for young people, but was forced out of her job because of her views.

gious and political controversy kept it out of the United States, even for testing, until 1994. Meanwhile, with little fanfare, some doctors had developed other combinations of pills to be used for the same purpose.

Even so, however, many young women became pregnant when they were still in their teens. Many women's groups tried to make up for the lack of information by providing it themselves. One classic example was the Boston Women's Health Collective, which first published its best-selling *Our Bodies, Ourselves* in 1973.

Physician Bernardine P. Healy was the first woman to head the National Institutes of Health (1991–1993).

Women's Health

Another related problem was that many areas of women's health had been ignored. Astonishingly, even in the late 20th century, much medical research on diseases and treatments had been done solely on males, with no females included.

That began to change only in the 1980s and 1990s. In the United States, physician Bernardine P. Healy (1944–) became the first woman to head the National Institutes of Health (1991–1993). Even before she was appointed, the NIH established an Office on Research on Women's Health, headed by physician Vivian Pinn. Its charge was to encourage research on women's health matters, and also to attract more women into medical careers.

Certainly far more women were moving into all levels of medicine in the late 20th century. They still met sexual discrimination in male-dominated hospitals and medical institutions, and many of the top jobs were still held by men. But women also moved into key positions. In 1989, Antonia C. Novello became the first woman surgeon general of the U.S. Public Health Service. Joycelyn Elders was named to the same post in 1993, but had to leave before term's end because of controversy over her support for sex education, including birth control information and access.

Physician Antonia C. Novello was the first woman to become surgeon general of the U.S. Public Health Service.

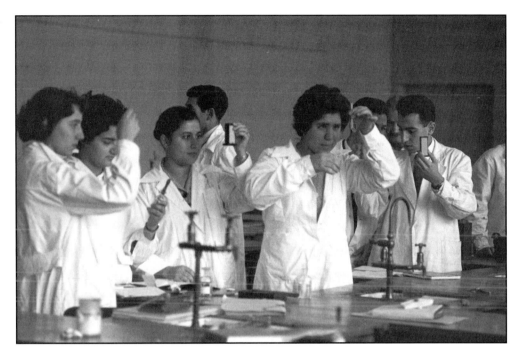

Women moved into medicine around the world. These students were learning how to do blood tests at the Medical College in Baghdad, Iraq.

Medical technology offered extraordinary new possibilities to women who had been unable to become pregnant. The whole range of what is now called *reproductive technology* began in 1977 with this seemingly simple procedure: Sperm and egg were mixed in a laboratory dish. If they fused to form a fertilized egg, this could then be implanted in a woman as the beginning of a pregnancy. The whole process is called *in vitro* ("in glass") fertilization.

Despite the many benefits of medical technology, many women felt that the process of pregnancy was being "medicalized." As a result the late 20th century saw two related shifts in childbirth. One was the spread of natural childbirth, seeking normal delivery through relaxation and breathing techniques, without the use of medications, except where necessary, and often with the father participating in the delivery.

The other was the return of midwifery, now often in the form of well-trained nurse-midwives. Some attended at deliveries in the home, and others in birthing centers. In many areas, midwives had difficulty winning acceptance in the medical community. However, their popularity forced hospitals to adopt some of their innovations. Many hospitals came to develop birth centers staffed by midwives and having a home-like atmosphere.

Social Control

Women in many developing countries had far more serious concerns relating to their bodies. Many millions of women were still being subjected to the practice of *genital mutilation*, also called female circumcision. The purpose is to destroy any possibility of sexual pleasure, but the women are

Roe v. Wade

In 1973, the U.S. Supreme Court legalized abortion in the United States, in the case of *Roe v. Wade* ruling that a pregnant woman had the right to choose to abort her unborn child before the fetus she was carrying became "viable." As a practical matter, the Court ruled that meant the pregnant woman could choose abortion without restriction in the first three months (trimester) of pregnancy, while states could regulate abortion but not prohibit it during the second three months. In the third trimester, states could regulate or prohibit abortion, unless the mother's life or health were in danger.

The decision opened a massive set of arguments and campaigns. On one side were those who favored a pregnant woman's right to choose an abortion (a *pro-choice* position, sometimes called *pro-abortion*). On the other were those against that right (the *antiabortion* or *pro-life* position). In the decades that followed, some antiabortion activists even bombed clin-

ics and murdered doctors who did abortions, though most antiabortion people condemned the murders of their opponents.

The Supreme Court modified its position several times. In the end, however, it reaffirmed its basic position legalizing abortion, in the case of *Planned Parenthood v. Casey*. The decision, specifically upholding the 1973 *Roe v. Wade* decision, was written by Justice Sandra Day O'Connor, who personally opposed abortion on moral grounds, but who wrote finally that:

Men and women of good conscience can disagree, and we suppose some always shall disagree, about the profound moral and spiritual implications of terminating a pregnancy, even in its earliest stages. Some of us as individuals find abortion offensive to our most basic principles of morality, but that cannot control our decision. Our obligation is to define the liberty of all, not to mandate our own moral code.

forced to live their lives in great pain, with great and wholly unnecessary health problems caused to themselves and their children. The practice is found in some African and western Asian countries, mostly Arab-Muslim, though it dates back to the pharaohs. It has been widely condemned internationally. One notable campaigner against the practice is Alice Walker (see "Writing Women," p. 96). In a landmark

case, the United States in 1996 granted asylum to Fauziya Kasinga, who had fled her native Togo in 1994 to escape ritual genital mutilation.

In many countries, especially those with huge populations, such as China and India, female children were still being killed or aborted before birth because of their sex. This has traditionally been called *female infanticide*, though it often now goes by the

Graphically demonstrating their views, these campaigners have a simple message: "Abortion Kills Children."

name of *son preference*. With the new scanning technology that allowed doctors to learn the sex of babies before actual birth, abortion of female babies became even more common, despite international efforts to ban the practice. The pressure of fast-growing populations and, in China, a "one-child" policy, increased the practice.

In some of these countries, also, women are subjected to forced sterilization (an operation to end the possibility of childbearing). In China, a woman who has already had one child may be jailed if she becomes

pregnant again, and released only after agreeing to abortion and sterilization.

Women in some countries taken over by radical Islamic fundamentalists have even more serious problems. In Afghanistan, in the late 1990s, the Taliban government barred all women from working. That included women physicians—but male physicians were barred from treating women patients. That left most women with no medical care at all—a situation darker than that at the depth of the Dark Ages.

In China, which had a "one-child" policy, a woman who had already had a child could sometimes be forced to have an abortion or have an operation to prevent her having more children.

Women in Science

Women continued to move into all the sciences in the late 20th century. Some of them would receive the world's top honors.

Pioneering biochemical researcher Barbara McClintock (1902–1992) won the 1983 Nobel Prize for physiology or medicine for her work on genetics. She had first announced her discovery that genetic fragments could "jump" within a cell in 1951—an idea ridiculed at the time.

Nuclear physicist Rosalyn Yalow (1921–) and internist Solomon A. Berson won the same prize in 1977 for their 1950 discovery of a way to use radioactive particles in the body for analysis and medical diagnosis. In 1976, Yalow had been the first woman

Above: *Nuclear physicist Rosalyn Yalow was cowinner of the 1977 Nobel Prize for physiology or medicine for helping to develop a way to use radioactive trace particles in medical diagnosis.*

Barbara McClintock won the 1983 Nobel Prize for physiology or medicine for her work in genetics—which people had laughed at in the 1940s.

ever to win the prestigious Albert Lasker Basic Medical Research Award.

Italian-American neurobiologist Rita Levi-Montalcini and Stanley Cohen won the 1987 Nobel Prize for physiology or medicine for their 1954 discovery of the nerve-growth factor. This substance stimulates the growth of nerve cells.

American biochemist Gertrude Elion (1918–) and two others shared the 1988 Nobel Prize for physiology or medicine for their development of drugs to treat diseases such as leukemia and AIDS.

American research chemist Stephanie L. Kwolek (1923–) was given the 1980 American Chemical Society Award for creative invention. Her most notable invention was Kevlar (1965), a stronger-than-steel synthetic fiber used in products as diverse as bulletproof vests and spacecraft.

French nuclear physicist Marguerite Catherine Perey (1909–1975) became the first woman member of France's Academy of Sciences, in 1962. She had worked with both Marie Curie (see Vol. 8, p. 92) and Irène Joliot-Curie (see "Women and the Atom," Vol. 9, p. 85), and like them would die from radiation exposure. Perey discovered the naturally radioactive element actirium K (which she called *francium*) in 1939.

British astronomer Jocelyn Bell (1943–) discovered pulsars, a type of pulsating astronomical object, in 1967, when she was a graduate student. Antony Hewish, her professor, won the 1974 Nobel Prize for physics for the discovery, but Bell was overlooked.

British astronomer Margaret Burbidge (1920–) became the first woman director of the Royal Observatory at Greenwich in 1972. However, she was not given the traditional title of Astronomer Royal. Four years later she became the first woman president of the American Astronomical Society, and in 1981 president of the American Association for the Advancement of Science.

In another pair of firsts, Julia Bowman Robinson (1919–1985) was the first woman president of the American Mathematical Society and the first woman mathematician elected to the National Academy of Sciences. In 1984, Cathleen Synge Morzwetz became the first woman director of the celebrated Courant Institute of Mathematical Sciences.

Women and the Environment

Many notable women scientists focused on the natural world in the late 20th cen-

Women and minorities were still uncommon in many hard scientific and technical fields, so this young woman chemical engineer was rather rare.

Jane Goodall studied chimpanzees in Tanzania from 1960. Here she and her then-husband Hugo Van Lawick, a Dutch documentary photographer, watched a friend examining a camera.

tury. One of the most widely influential was Rachel Carson (see p. 87).

Through her decades of studying chimpanzees in Tanzania, from 1960, Jane Goodall (1934–) has contributed enormously to our understanding of them and their habitat. Through her books and films, she also helped many people understand the complicated relationships among beings in the natural world.

Similarly, Dian Fossey (1932–1985) began studying mountain gorillas in Rwanda in 1967. Her book *Gorillas in the Mist* (1983) was the basis for a film.

Austrian conservationist Joy Gessner Adamson (1910–1980) also won a wide audience for her book *Born Free* (1960), about how she prepared her lion cub Elsa for a life in the wild. She founded the World Wildlife Fund in the U.S.A. in 1962.

Like Rachel Carson, many women were drawn to marine biology. American marine biologist Sylvia Earle Mead (1935–) was the only woman on a 60-person diving team exploring life on the floor of the Indian Ocean in 1964. But six years later she led the first all-woman underwater expedition, a two-week mission near the Virgin Islands.

Many other women were active in trying to preserve the earth from threats to the environment. A key international envrionmental leader, Petra Kelly (1947–1992) co-founded the German Green Party, which became a political force in Germany. British economist Barbara Ward (Baroness Jackson of Lodsworth; 1914–1981) focused

Dian Fossey studied mountain gorillas in Rwanda from 1967 until her murder there in 1985.

Rachel Carson and the Green Movement

In 1962, biologist, ecologist, teacher, and writer Rachel Louise Carson (1907–1964) wrote one of the most influential books of the 20th century. It was *Silent Spring*, her landmark work on the tremendous damage being done to life on Earth by toxic pesticides. Her greatest focus was on DDT (dichloro-diphenol-trichloro-ethane), then the most widely used pesticide in the world by far. She established beyond doubt that DDT was highly toxic to fish and even more deadly for birds, since it thinned their egg shells. That caused birds to be unable to reproduce and brought many species close to extinction, among them the bald eagle and peregrine falcon. Carson's work was a worldwide wake-up call. DDT was banned in the U.S. in 1972 and then in many other countries, though it continues to be used in some countries, causing enormous damage.

Carson's work did far more than trigger the DDT ban. It raised the right worldwide issues at the right time, when people in many countries were beginning to be deeply concerned about the damage being caused by unrestrained use of toxic chemicals and other toxic substances in the environment. She was one of the first to warn that the environment and all the lifeforms in it were in great and increasing danger, and so was a major force in generating what became the worldwide environmental movement.

Carson was trained as a marine biologist. Even before *Silent Spring* she had come to wide public view with her best-selling book *The Sea Around Us* (1951).

Rachel Carson

on more equal distribution of the world's resources. She was president, then chair, of the International Institute for Environment and Development from 1973 until her death. In the United States, Carol Browner (1955–) became a key environmentalist as head of the Environmental Protection Agency (1993–).

Some women focused on alerting the world to specific hazards. From 1978, Lois Gibbs led the campaign to close Love Canal, a toxic waste dump in Niagara Falls,

New York. Organizing to help others facing similar problems, she founded the Citizen's Clearinghouse for Hazardous Wastes in 1981.

Karen Gay Silkwood (1946–1974) was concerned with health and safety hazards in the plant where she worked on atomic materials. She died in a highly questionable automobile accident as she was en route to meet a *New York Times* reporter. The papers she had with her were never found.

On a far different time scale, British anthropologist and paleontologist Mary Leakey (1913–1996) helped transform think-

Sylvia Mead (center) is shown with the other four members of the first all-woman underwater expedition in 1970. They were celebrating the end of their two weeks on the ocean floor.

Karen Silkwood was concerned about radiation safety hazards at the plutonium plant where she worked. She later died suspiciously in an automobile accident.

ing about human revolution, working at Olduvai Gorge, in Tanzania, with her husband, Louis Leakey, and son, Richard Leakey. Lithuanian-American archaeologist Marija Gimbutas (1920–1994) was a key supporter of the theory that mother-goddess worship was widespread among early cultures (see "Venus Figurines and Mother Goddesses," Vol. 1, p. 14).

For more information on these aspects of women's lives, see the Science, Technology, and Medicine sections of other volumes in this set. You can also look up specific topics, such as "medicine" or "astronomy," in the Master Index to the set, at the end of each volume. See also the bibliography page at the end of each volume.

Illustrated History of Women

Arts and Literature

Writing Women

For women writers, the world opened far wider than ever before in the last four decades of the 20th century. In many countries, among them the United States, Canada, Britain, France, and most other western European countries, women reached wider audiences and commanded greater respect. In much of the world, however, women still had great difficulty getting their work published and so reaching their audiences. Translation also tended to run one way. Well-known Western authors such as Toni Morrison of the United States and Marguerite Duras of France would be translated into many languages, while authors such as Mariama Ba of Senegal, Ama Ata

Above: *A full 47 years after her first novel was published, Dorothy West—a survivor from the Harlem Renaissance—published her second,* The Wedding *(1995), to much acclaim.*

Toni Morrison won the Nobel Prize for literature in 1983, the first African-American woman, and the second American woman, to do so.

Winner of the 1993 Nobel Prize for literature, Nadine Gordimer was known for her explorations of the lives of people in a South Africa badly corrupted by racism.

Aidoo of Senegal, and Grace Ogot of Tanzania were translated far less often.

Nobel Honors

Several women were awarded the Nobel Prize for literature in the late 20th century. One of them was Toni Morrison (1931–), who in 1993 became the first African-American woman and the second American woman to win the literature Nobel. A teacher of literature and then an editor, Morrison's work includes the novels *The Bluest Eye* (1970), *Sula* (1973), *Song of Solomon* (1977), *Tar Baby* (1981), *Beloved* (1987; it won a Pulitzer Prize), and *Jazz* (1992).

South African novelist and short story writer Nadine Gordimer (1923–) won the 1991 Nobel Prize for literature. Much of her work has focused on the lives of people living in a South African society dominated and stained by the corrupt racist system of *apartheid* during the decades before South Africa became a multiracial democracy (see "Women and Civil Rights," p. 22). Often called the "conscience of South Africa," Gordimer was during the apartheid period directly politically active and was a founder of the multiracial Congress of South African Writers.

Terry McMillan had a major hit with her novel Waiting to Exhale, *but she had to go on the road to get bookstores to stock and sell her earlier work.*

cused on oddities of everyday life. The Nobel committee called her the "Mozart of poetry."

Writing about Women's Lives

The work of many women authors in the late 20th century reflects intense concern with the quality of women's lives. That is certainly so for the work of African-American author Maya Angelou (1928–), whose first major work was the autobiographical *I Know Why the Caged Bird Sings* (1970). Her further works all focused on the same personal themes, including those that dealt with the lives of other women, as in her 1995 work *Phenomenal Woman: Four Poems Celebrating Women*. In 1992 Angelou reached an audience of tens of millions when she read

Joyce Carol Oates was one of the most prolific and most respected writers of the late 20th century.

German poet and playwright Nelly Sachs (1891–1970) shared the 1966 Nobel Prize for literature with Shmuel Yoseph Agnon. Sachs's work dealt with the murder of millions of Jews by the Germans during the Holocaust. Her powerful and moving poetry collections included *In the Dwellings of Death* (1946), *And No One Knows Where to Go* (1957), and *Flight and Metamorphosis* (1959).

Polish poet Wislawa Szymborska (1923–) won the 1996 Nobel Prize for literature. Her award was something of a surprise, for she was somewhat reclusive, and her work had until then been little known outside Poland. At first political, her work later fo-

Ursula K. Le Guin has won wide acclaim for her science fiction novels.

Ruth Prawer Jhabvala is a widely published novelist, but she is probably best known as a screenwriter, especially for Merchant-Ivory productions. Director James Ivory took this photograph.

her poem "On the Pulse of the Morning," at President Bill Clinton's first inauguration, becoming the first inaugural poet since 1961.

The work of Sylvia Plath (1932–1963) has been seen by many as a single long scream of anguish, speaking to the concerns of many other women of her time. That is especially true of her only novel, the autobiographical *The Bell Jar* (1963), as well as many of her poems. Much of her poetry, including her Pulitzer Prize–winning *Collected Poems* (1981), was published after she committed suicide.

Canadian writer Margaret Atwood (1939–) has focused on women's lives, including feminist concerns. Her best-known novels include *The Edible Woman* (1969), *Surfacing* (1973), *Life Before Man* (1979), *The Handmaid's Tale* (1986), and *Alias Grace* (1996). *The Handmaid's Tale*, set in a fictional future society in which women have become merely breeders, was adapted into the 1990 film.

British author Muriel Spark (1918–) is best known for her novel *The Prime of Miss Jean Brodie* (1961), set in a Scottish girls' school, basis of the 1968 film that brought

Canadian writer Margaret Atwood is best known for The Handmaid's Tale, *basis for the film.*

Maggie Smith an Academy Award. Her other books, many of them focusing on women's lives, include *The Girls of Slender Means* (1963) and *A Far Cry from Kensington* (1988). British author Margaret Drabble (1939–) has focused on the emotional lives of women in modern society, in such novels as *The Garrick Year* (1964) and *In the Realms of Gold* (1975).

African-American novelist and poet Alice Walker (1944–) has primarily explored the lives of African-American women, especially focusing on the sexism and racism they encountered. A feminist—or, as she calls it, "womanist"—Walker had her greatest success with her novel *The Color Purple* (1982), which describes the life of an African-American woman in the American South, basis of the 1985 film starring Whoopi Goldberg and Oprah Winfrey. Walker also expressed interest in women's lives in more directly political ways. Walker took up the genital mutilation of women in her novel *Possessing the Secret of Joy* (1992), as well as in a 1993 film and a nonfiction book, *Warrior Marks: Female Genital Mutilation and the Sexual Blinding of Women*, written with Pratibha Parmar. She also directly campaigned for an end to the practice (see "Women's Bodies, Women's Lives," p. 78).

Other Views

Women's lives and political matters have been mixed in the works of several other leading women authors. Rhodesian-born British writer Doris Lessing (1919–) became a leading author starting with her first Africa-set novel, *The Grass Was Singing* (1950), though her best-known work is *The Golden Notebook* (1962). For her political views, often expressed through her novels, she was banned from White-run, racist Rhodesia (now Zimbabwe).

Another highly political writer, who merged the political and emotional sides of life, was French writer and director Marguerite Duras (1914–1996). Of her many screenplays, she was most famous for the first: *Hiroshima, Mon Amour* (1959), a love story set in the Japanese city of Hiroshima after the atomic bomb was exploded there during World War II. Among her novels were *The Sea Wall* (1950), *The Sailor from Gibraltar* (1952), and the worldwide best-

Doris Lessing's writings were so controversial in White-dominated, racist Rhodesia that for many years she was barred from visiting her homeland.

Mona Van Duyn was the first woman to be named poet laureate of the United States, in 1992.

seller *The Lover* (1984), a love story set in Vietnam (then French-occupied Indochina), basis for the 1992 film.

British writer Iris Murdoch (1919–) has mixed fiction and philosophy in her work. She is best known for her novels, including *The Sandcastle* (1957), *The Severed Head* (1961), and *The Green Knight* (1993).

New Zealand author Janet Frame (1924–) largely writes of what she sees as a kind of insanity under the surface of ordinary life. Her novels include *Owls Do Cry* (1957), *Yellow Flowers in an Antipodean Room* (1968), and *Living in the Maniototo* (1979).

American writer Joan Didion (1934–) often writes of the lives of women facing a deadly, menacing world. Among her best-known works are the essay collection *Slouching Toward Bethlehem* (1969), and the

novels *Play It As It Lays* (1970) and *The Last Thing He Wanted* (1996).

Two women poets were honored in the United States in the 1990s. Mona Van Duyn (1921–) was the first woman to become U.S. poet laureate, in 1992. That same year, she won a Pulitzer Prize for her poetry collection *Near Changes*. She was succeeded in 1993 by Rita Dove (1952–), who was the first African-American poet laureate. Dove's 1986 poetry collection *Thomas and Beulah* had won a Pulitzer Prize.

These are just a few of the many women writers who found voices and audiences in the late 20th century. For many writers of fiction, like some of those mentioned above, movies and television have brought even wider audiences around the world.

Like e. e. cummings, American writer bell hooks prefers to have no capital letters in her name.

On Stage and Screen

In the final decades of the 20th century, the balance between the screen entertainment forms and the live theater had long since shifted to the screen. The theater was far from dead, but film and television were large, worldwide industries. Cable television had come and was challenging the networks, while total world television audiences had expanded enormously. American films were more and more dominant around the world. The Internet had come. The whole international communications and entertainment industry was in the process of merging, with huge international companies competing for control of world markets.

In that new world, power and control still rested in male-dominated companies and the people, banks, and investment houses that controlled them. However, international movie and television stars—who commanded huge audiences—also held a great deal of power, enough so that they were no longer entirely the captives of these companies.

Women who were major stars in film and television were able to make their own "deals," with some going far beyond acting and singing to become filmmakers and run production companies. Unlike the major companies, however, most such stars were able to enjoy real independence and strength only as long as their popularity continued.

Powers That Be

One of the most notable of the new, independent "megastars" is African-American talk show host Oprah Winfrey (1954–).

Above: *A star in theater from childhood, Helen Hayes built a career in film and television late in her life.*

people in the world, earning more than $150 million a year.

Several other women stars, who worked mainly in television, became extremely popular performers, and in the process developed some economic strength—although that strength was not enough to guarantee their future as performers. One of these was Mary Tyler Moore (1936–), who played Mary Richards, a very independent career woman, in her own "The Mary Tyler Moore Show" (1970–1977). Another was veteran British character actress Angela Lansbury (1925–), who on television starred as Cabot Cove amateur detective Jessica

Long a supporting player on film, Angela Lansbury became a star in the theater and on television, in her long-running series "Murder, She Wrote."

After a start as a television reporter, Winfrey became a star daytime television talk show host in the mid-1980s, in her own "Oprah Winfrey Show." She built that show into an institution, as the highest-rated of all daytime television shows. She developed such a massive, extraordinarily devoted audience that she had only to recommend a book to make it a runaway best-seller. She was also able to make herself into a big business, taking full control of her own financial arrangements. In the process, she made herself one of the highest-paid

Mary Tyler Moore was most identified with the independent career woman Mary Richards, whom she played on "The Mary Tyler Moore Show" (1970–1977).

Almost 40 years after she starred in My Fair Lady *(1956), Julie Andrews returned to Broadway in 1995 to star in* Victor, Victoria, *as a woman pretending to be a man pretending to be a woman.*

Fletcher in the long-running hit show "Murder, She Wrote" (1984–1996).

One of the greatest superstars of the modern era is Barbra Streisand (1942–), whose career has spanned theater, music, films, and television. She made her first major breakthrough on stage, in *I Can Get It for You Wholesale* (1962), and won a best actress Academy Award playing Fanny Brice in *Funny Girl* (1964), which she had played on stage a year before. In the mid-1960s, she became an international superstar as a popular music stylist and has remained so for the rest of the century, winning six Grammy Awards as best vocalist. At the same time, she starred in many theater and television films. Throughout her career, Streisand has also pushed hard to go beyond performing to become a producer, director, and composer who is able to take charge of her own creative life. As early as 1976, she produced and starred in the film *A Star Is Born*. She went on to direct, produce, and star in *Yentl* (1983), and to direct and star in *The Prince of Tides* (1991). In 1996, she expanded her scope even further, directing, producing, composing, starring, and singing in the film *The Mirror Has Two Faces*.

A stage star in mid-century, often playing with her husband, Hume Cronyn (left), Jessica Tandy won new stardom on film with her Oscar-winning performance in Driving Miss Daisy *(1989).*

Maryann Plunkett won a Tony for her starring role in Me and My Girl *(1984), later going on to play St. Joan on Broadway.*

Another great star who has expanded her career to include far more than performing is actress, director, and producer Jodie Foster (1962–). She first became a star as a child actress in Hollywood, especially opposite Robert De Niro in *Taxi Driver*. As an adult, her major breakthrough came in her Academy Award–winning role in *Accused* (1988). She won a second best actress Academy Award in the worldwide hit *The Silence of the Lambs* (1991), opposite Anthony Hopkins as "Hannibal the Cannibal" Lecter. Foster's first major directing effort was the film *Little Man Tate* (1992), in which she also starred. She also coproduced and starred in *Nell* (1994) and directed *Home for the Holidays* (1995).

Women Directors

In the late 20th century, the world also began to open somewhat more to women directors and producers who were not performers—for in the world of work, sexual discrimination was under attack and women were more successfully fighting for equality of opportunity (see "Women at Work," p. 47).

Though there were still relatively few women directors, compared to the number of males, there were many more than earlier in the century. Among them were such directors as Penny Marshall, who directed *A League of Their Own* (1992); Martha Coolidge, whose work included *Rambling Rose* (1991); and New Zealand director Jane Campion, who directed *The Piano* (1993). Some notable directors from a slightly earlier period were Lina Wertmuller, who made several top Italian films in the 1970s, including *Seven Beauties* (1976); Joan Micklin Silver, who directed *Hester Street* (1975); and Nelly Kaplan, whose documentary film *Le Regard Picasso* won a Golden Lion award at the 1967 Venice Film Festival.

Movie Stars

Beyond these were many other great women film stars. Of these we can mention only a few here.

Roseanne Barr Arnold, later simply called Roseanne, went from being on welfare to starring in a top hit series on television, "Roseanne" (1988–1997).

Meryl Streep (1949–) won a best actress Academy Award for *Sophie's Choice* (1982), and best supporting actress Academy Award for *Kramer vs. Kramer* (1980). Jane Fonda (1937–) won best actress Academy Awards for *Klute* (1971) and *Coming Home* (1978). The daughter of actor Henry Fonda, she received as much attention for her opposition to the Vietnam War as for her superb acting.

Whoopi Goldberg (1950–) was one of the few African-American women to become a top Hollywood star late in the century. Her films included *The Color Purple* (1986), based on Alice Walker's 1982 novel, and *Ghost* (1990), for which she won a best supporting actress Oscar as a Harlem-based psychic.

British actress and writer Emma Thompson (1959–) received a best actress Academy Award for *Howard's End* (1992). Also a writer, she adapted Jane Austen's *Sense and Sensibility* for the 1995 film, in which she starred as well. Another notable British film star is Julie Christie, who won a best actress Academy Award for *Darling* (1965), and in the same year starred as Lara in *Dr. Zhivago*.

Across the English Channel, French actress Catherine Deneuve (1943–) became a great international star in *The Umbrellas of*

Ellen DeGeneres broke new ground in 1997 when she "came out" as a lesbian, both on her hit television series "Ellen" and in her private life.

Cherbourg (1963). She would remained so for the rest of the century.

Stars in the Theater

Many great artists continued to make the theater a major part of their work, even though some may have become better known in television and films. One example was stage and screen star Glenn Close (1947–). She became a major film star, starting with *The World According to Garp* (1982), while also winning best actress Tony Awards for *The Real Thing* (1984), *Death and the Maiden* (1992), and *Sunset Boulevard* (1993).

Another wide-ranging star was British actress Glenda Jackson (1936–). She won best actress Academy Awards for *Sunday, Bloody Sunday* (1971) and *A Touch of Class* (1973), and was an extraordinary Queen Elizabeth I in the television miniseries *Elizabeth R* (1971). She was also a major figure on the British stage for almost 30 years, until retiring in 1992 after winning election as a Labour member of Parliament.

Another great actress who took on a political role was Jane Alexander (1939–). She is best known for her starring roles on stage and screen in *The Great White Hope* (1968; 1970) and on television as Eleanor Roosevelt in *Eleanor and Franklin* (1976). She

A notable actress, especially in the theater, Jane Alexander helped preserve federal funding for the arts during her years as head of the National Endowment for the Arts (1993–1997).

A wide-ranging actress, Shirley MacLaine also toured as a dancer and wrote several best-selling books.

played a major role in preserving federal funding for the arts, however, as head of the National Endowment for the Arts (1993–1997).

The late 20th century saw some other great stage actresses. One of them was Colleen Dewhurst (1926–1991). She won best actress Tony Awards for *All the Way Home* (1960) and *A Moon for the Misbegotten* (1973), one of the several Eugene O'Neill plays in which she starred.

British actress Vanessa Redgrave (1937–) has been a great international stage and screen star for more than 30 years. Among her many notable roles were in *The Prime of Miss Jean Brodie* on stage (1966) and in *Isadora* (1968) on screen. She was the daughter of actor Michael Redgrave and actress Rachel Kempson, the sister of actress Lynn

Redgrave and actor Corin Redgrave, and the mother of actress Natasha Richardson—one of several actresses in that third generation.

Several notable actresses have been associated with the Royal Shakespeare Company in Britain. Among them are Judi Dench (1934–), a major figure in the British theater, and South African actor and director Janet Suzman (1939–).

American actress Lauren Bacall (1924–) was a film star early in her career, often opposite her husband, Humphrey Bogart. However, later in her career she became a star on Broadway, winning best actress Tony Awards in *Applause* (1970) and *Woman of the Year* (1981).

Laura Dern was nominated for an Academy Award for her performance in Martha Coolidge's film Rambling Rose *(1991).*

Music and Dance

In the late 20th century, music became an ever more important part of the whole mix of media. Now, as before, a composer-singer might write a song, and see it become a worldwide hit on stage, screen, tour, and record. But now there were even more possibilities. A movie soundtrack might go right to the top of the charts, becoming a worldwide hit from that direction. A song might become a hit video or be played hundreds of thousands of times over the Internet. Young artists like Brandy (1979–) and LeAnn Rimes (1982–) might become international celebrities overnight. Established artists like Bonnie Raitt (1949–) might see their careers take off again with a single unexpected hit, as she did with the album *Nick of Time* (1989).

Above: *Like many artists of the 1990s, Brandy was both a singer and an actress, with hit records as well as a television series, "Moesha."*

Longtime recording star Bonnie Raitt took her career to new heights with her 1989 album Nick of Time, *which brought her numerous awards.*

Whitney Houston became a major international singing star right from her first album, Whitney Houston *(1985), later also building a film career.*

In the late 20th century, none of the era's popular and jazz singers reached the commanding popularity of such earlier singers as Ella Fitzgerald (see Vol. 9, p. 106) and Billie Holiday (see "Music and Dance," Vol. 9, p. 103), even though some sold far more records. However, some have come close. African-American singer Whitney Houston (1963–), for example, has built an enormous worldwide audience for her work, starting with her first album, *Whitney Houston* (1985). Extending her career into films, Houston starred opposite Kevin Costner in *The Bodyguard* (1992). The film's soundtrack sold more than 16 million copies, becoming the top soundtrack album ever and illustrating the power of the new forms in which people bought and listened to music. Many of her songs also became hit music videos.

Another top popular artist was singer and actress Madonna (1958–), who first became an international celebrity in the early 1980s. She held on to huge worldwide audiences through the late 1990s, with a combination of highly publicized concert tours, records, and films. Such early albums as *Like a Virgin* (1983) and *True Blue* (1986) were worldwide hits, as were such concert tours as her "Blond Ambition" concert tour,

Madonna became one of the biggest international celebrities of the 1980s as a singer, maintaining her celebrity into the 1990s, as she also built a film career.

Tracey Chapman became a widely popular writer and singer of protest songs, starting with her first album, Tracy Chapman *(1988).*

African-American singer and actress Diana Ross (1944–) was the lead singer of The Supremes in the 1960s. She became a great star as a solo performer in concert and recordings from the 1970s.

The folk revival of the 1960s also had its share of stars. Among the most notable was folk singer and guitarist Joan Baez (1941–). A leading civil rights movement and anti-war activist, she was in the 1960s and 1970s perhaps best known for her rendition of "We Shall Overcome." Another major

following her film role as Breathless Mahoney in *Dick Tracy* (1990). Most of her film appearances were in straight dramatic, rather than singing roles, as in *A League of Their Own* (1992).

Many women who were still major stars late in the century first emerged in the 1960s. African-American singer Aretha Franklin (1942–), a gospel and rhythm-and-blues singer, became the leading soul singer of her day. She was known as the "Queen of Soul" during the late 1960s and early 1970s, when she became a great figure in the civil rights movement, especially for her rendition of "Amazing Grace" (1972).

Diana Ross led The Supremes in the 1960s, then became an individual recording star from the 1970s.

Judy Collins was a major figure in the folk movement of the 1960s, starting with her first album, A Maid of Constant Sorrow *(1961).*

American folk singer and social activist was Judy Collins (1939–), from her first album *A Maid of Constant Sorrow* (1961).

Canadian folksinger, composer, and guitarist Joni Mitchell (1943–) emerged in the same period. She was tremendously popular in the 1960s and 1970s, and made a notable comeback in the mid-1990s.

The same period also saw the emergence of blues singer Janis Joplin (1943–1970). Her death from a heroin overdose was both caution and emblem for the '60s generation.

In the world of country music, singer and songwriter Loretta Lynn (1935–) was a leading figure. She was most identified with her autobiographical song "Coal Miner's Daughter" (1970), also the title of her 1976 autobiography and of the 1988 film, star-

ring an Oscar-winning Sissy Spacek as Lynn.

Dolly Parton (1946–) was a country music singing star from the early 1970s. However, she may have had her greatest impact as a songwriter. Among her many songs was "I Will Always Love You," turned into an all-time top hit by Whitney Houston in *The Bodyguard*.

In a very different style, merging country and popular styles, was k. d. lang (1962–). She was one of the first openly lesbian performers to win wide popular audiences.

The first African-American Miss America, Vanessa Williams overcame the controversy over her resignation from that position to build a career as a singer and actress.

More on the popular music side, Cher (1946–) became a singing star in the 1960s in Sonny and Cher, with her then-husband Sonny Bono. After going on her own in 1975, she became a major solo star and also became a highly respected actress, winning an Academy Award for best actress for *Moonstruck* (1987).

One of the leading concert and recording artists of the early 1990s was singer Mariah Carey (1970–). Her major career started with her album *Mariah Carey* (1990).

Vanessa Williams (1963–) was the first African-American Miss America (1983), until forced to resign after *Penthouse* magazine printed some nude photographs of her. She went on to build a strong career as a singer and actress in theater, television, and films.

One of the most popular singers worldwide was Teresa Teng (1953–1995). The Taiwanese singer performed in concert and on recordings to hundreds of millions of fans throughout east and southeast Asia. She retired to France in 1989 after sharply criticizing the massacre of pro-democracy protesters in China's Tienanmen Square.

Classical Music

In the male-dominated world of opera, one very rare figure was U.S. opera company director, conductor, and producer Sarah Caldwell (1924–). She had founded the Opera Company of Boston (1958) and was later the first woman to conduct at the Metropolitan Opera (1976).

Another very unusual figure was U.S. soprano and opera director Beverly Sills (1929–). A star in world opera during the 1970s, she became director of the New York City Opera in 1979.

The late 20th century saw a number of major woman opera singers. One was African-American soprano Leontyne Price (1927–), a worldwide star from the mid-1950s, and a star at the Metropolitan from 1961 until her retirement in 1985. Another was Metropolitan Opera soprano Roberta Peters (1930–). Another was New Zealand

Leontyne Price was one of the first African-American singers to be fully accepted in grand opera, becoming a major international star.

soprano Kiri Te Kanawa (1944–), a great international star and also a popular recording artist.

Women continued to move into classical music as instrumentalists. By the 1990s, at least 25 percent of the members of major classical orchestras in the United States were women. However, resistance to women continued to be much stronger in many European orchestras.

Classical conductors continued to be few and far between. The rare women in this position included British conductor Jane Glover, French conductor Cathcrine Comet, and Zeng Ziaoying, China's first woman conductor.

More women soloists did emerge late in the century. Their numbers were not large, but included some major individual artists. Notable among them was the great British cellist Jacqueline Du Pré (1945–1987), whose career was cut short by multiple sclerosis. Spanish pianist Alicia De Larrocha and Japanese violinist Midori, among many others, also built major careers in this period.

The composing side of classical music presented a somewhat better picture for women than it had earlier in the century. Even so, only a few women composers were as yet recognized as substantial figures in the world of classical music. One major figure was U.S. composer Ellen Taaffe Zwilich (1939–), who in 1983 became the first woman to win a Pulitzer Prize for music, for her Symphony No. 1 (1982). A second was Shulamit Ran, who in 1991 was the first woman to become a composer-in-residence at a top United States orchestra, the Chicago Symphony. Among the best known of the new generation of women composers in

classical music late in the century were Australian composer Alison Bauld; British composer Nicola LeFanu, daughter of composer Elizabeth Maconchy; Scottish composers Thea Musgrave and Judith Weir; Polish composer Marta Ptaszynska; and United States composers Joan Tower, Barbara Kolb, and Nancy Van de Vere.

Dance

In modern dance, Martha Graham (see "Music and Dance," Vol. 9, p. 103) continued to be a dominant figure until her death in 1991. She was still choreographing until a year before her death; her *Maple Leaf Rag* made its debut in New York in October 1990. In 1991, she published her autobiography, *Blood Memory*.

Paula Abdul was known as a dancer and choreographer, for Michael Jackson among others, before making the unusual move to her own career as a recording artist.

Long the leading dancer with the Alvin Ailey Dance Company, Judith Jamison returned to lead the troupe after Ailey's death.

Among the later women in modern dance, Twyla Tharp (1941–) was a leading dancer and choreographer. Her work often carried jazz themes, in such modern classics as *The Bix Pieces* (1972), *Eight Jelly Rolls* (1976), and *Push Comes to Shove* (1976). She also choreographed several films, among them *Hair* (1979) and *White Nights* (1985).

Another major figure in dance was African-American dancer and choreographer Judith Jamison (1944–). She was the leading dancer in the Alvin Ailey Company (1967–1980), focusing in her work on African-American dance themes. After Ailey's death, in 1990, she rejoined the company as its artistic director and choreographer.

In classical ballet, Margot Fonteyn (1919–1991) continued to be the prima ballerina of Britain's Royal Ballet, and one of the world's leading ballerinas. In 1962, she began her celebrated dancing partnership with Soviet dancer Rudolf Nureyev, who had defected to the West in 1961. They would dance together until her retirement in 1979. Soviet dancer Maya Plisetskaya (1925–), prima ballerina of Moscow's Bolshoi Ballet, continued to be one of the world's leading ballerinas. Other leading ballerinas included Soviet dancer Natalia Makarova, who defected to the West in 1970, and U.S. ballerina Suzanne Farrell, who premiered several works of George Balanchine from the mid-1960s.

Margot Fonteyn was for many years the prima ballerina of Britain's Royal Ballet, here dancing in Swan Lake.

Visual Arts

Many highly regarded women worked in the late-20th-century visual arts, but few achieved major recognition in what was still largely a male-dominated world. One towering figure was Georgia O'Keeffe (1887–1986), who continued to develop her tremendous body of work, focusing on the huge sky and land of the American West, with color, light, and often highly abstracted forms. Now later in her long life, she produced such masterpieces as *The Winter Road* (1963) and her massive *Sky Above Clouds IV* (1965).

British sculptor Barbara Hepworth (1903–1975) also produced some of her greatest work in this period, such as her monumental *Single Form* (1961–1962), the

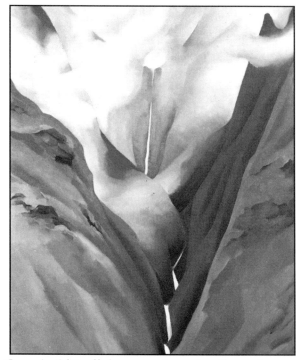

Above: *Wilhelmina Cole Holladay helped bring women's art to greater audiences, as founder and board chair of the National Museum of Women in the Arts.*

Georgia O'Keeffe became a towering figure in 20th-century art, increasingly drawn to abstract landscapes. This is her Waterfall No. III Iao Valley.

memorial to United Nations secretary-general Dag Hammarskjöld at New York's UN Plaza. Another major work by Hepworth was the sculpture *Square Stones with Circles* (1963).

Another major sculptor, an international figure from the 1950s, was Louise Nevelson (1900–1988), who began to work in a wide range of materials, among them plastic, aluminum, and steel, most notably in wall sculptures. As her career developed, her interest in environmental and outdoor sculptures grew. Another key artist of the time was French-American sculptor Louise Bourgeois (1911–), whose work was most notable for its fantasy forms. A third celebrated woman artist was painter Helen Frankenthaler (1928–), whose work and teaching greatly influenced many of the younger women artists of the period.

One of the most notable new artists of the period was architect and sculptor Maya Lin (1960–). In 1982 she created the extraordinarily successful Vietnam Veterans Memorial, in Washington, D.C. Her straightforward, simple black wall, carrying the names of those Americans who died in Vietnam, immediately became a national shrine, drawing millions of visitors. In 1989, Lin created the Civil Rights Movement memorial in Montgomery, Alabama.

Among the political feminists working in the visual arts, Judy Chicago (1939–) was a notable figure. She was best known by far for her large exhibition *The Dinner Party* (1978), a group work portraying her view of women's history. Another of her major works was *The Birth Project* (1989), aimed at portraying the role played by women in the creation of life.

Women artists made a considerable step forward in 1987, when the National Museum of Women in the Arts opened in Washington, D.C. It had been founded in 1981, with Wilhelmina Cole Holladay as president of its board of directors.

This is one of Louise Nevelson's famous wall sculptures, An American Tribute to the British People (Gold Wall) *(1950–1965).*

For more information on these aspects of women's lives, see the Arts and Literature sections of other volumes in this set. You can look up specific topics, such as "opera" or "visual arts," in the Master Index to the set, provided at the end of each volume. See also the bibliography page at the end of each volume.

Further Reading: 1960–1998

Many general books on women—including histories, chronologies, books of biographies, and works on various aspects of women's lives—are listed in Volume 1 (see p. 104). The books below are some additional works that focus on women in the late 20th century.

Belford, Barbara. *Brilliant Bylines: A Biographical Anthology of Notable Newspaperwomen in America.* New York: Columbia University Press, 1986.

Cant, Bob, and Susan Henning, eds. *Radical Records: 30 Years of Lesbian and Gay History.* London: Routledge, 1988.

Carabillo, Toni, et al. *Feminist Chronicles: 1953–1993.* Los Angeles: Women's Graphics, 1993.

Chafe, William H. *The Paradox of Change: American Women in the 20th Century.* New York: Oxford University Press, 1991. A revision of *The American Woman: Her Changing Social, Economic, and Political Roles, 1920–1970* (1972).

Clark, Judith Freeman. *Almanac of American Women in the 20th Century.* New York: Prentice Hall, 1987.

Davis, Flora. *Moving the Mountain: The Women's Movement in America Since 1960.* New York: Simon & Schuster, 1991.

Duby, Georges, and Michelle Perrot, gen. eds. *A History of Women.* Cambridge, MA: Belknap. *Vol. V: Toward a Cultural Identity in the 20th Century.* Françoise Thebaud and Georges Duby, eds. 1994.

Edwards, Julia. *Women of the World: The Great Foreign Correspondents.* Boston: Houghton Mifflin, 1988.

Faderman, Lillian. *Odd Girls and Twilight Lovers: A History of Lesbian Life in Twentieth-Century America.* New York: Columbia University Press, 1991.

Foner, Philip S. *Women and the American Labor Movement. Vol. 2: From World War I to the Present.* New York: Free Press, 1980.

Hardy, Gayle J. *American Women Civil Rights Activists: Biobibliographies of 68 Leaders, 1825–1992.* Jefferson, NC: McFarland, 1993.

Kaptur, Marcy. *Women of Congress: A Twentieth-Century Odyssey.* Washington, DC: Congressional Quarterly, 1996.

Litoff, Judy Barrett. *American Midwives: 1860 to the Present.* Westport, CT: Greenwood, 1978.

Rupp, Leila J., and Verta Taylor. *Survival in Doldrums: The American Women's Rights Movement, 1945 to the 1960's.* New York: Oxford University Press, 1987.

Smith, Harold L., ed. *British Feminism in the Twentieth Century.* Amherst: University of Massachusetts Press, 1990.

Woolum, Janet. *Outstanding Women Athletes: Who They Are and How They Influenced Sports in America.* Phoenix: Oryx, 1992.

Master Index

Note: Figures in bold are the volume numbers; the other figures are the page numbers. An asterisk (*) indicates that an image of the person is shown on the page(s) indicated.

A

Abbott, Berenice **9:** 111
Abbott, Edith **8:** 53, 58
Abbott, Grace **8:** 52-53*
Abbott, Margaret **8:** 72
Abdul, Paula **10:** 108
Abelard, Peter **2:** 33*
Abella **2:** 95
Abington, Frances **5:** 102
abortion **1:** 53; **9:** 75; **10:** 19, 61, 78-79, 82-83
Abzug, Bella **10:** 27, 33*
Academy Awards **8:** 105; **9:** 92, 96, 98-99, 103; **10:** 98-100
Acarie, Barbe **4:** 18
Acton, Elizabeth **6:** 40
Adams, Abigail **5:** 13-15; 23, 26-27*
Adams, Annette **8:** 19
Adams, Elizabeth **6:** 95
Adams, Harriet **8:** 58
Adams, Sharon **10:** 76
Adamson, Joy **10:** 86
Addams, Jane **7:** 36; **8:** 23, 31-32*, 52*
Adela, St. **2:** 13
Adelaide, St. **2:** 13
Adelaide, queen of Italy **2:** 18, 81
Aelflaed **2:** 12-13
Aethelflaed **2:** 81
African-Americans **1:** 29; **5:** 61-64, 99-101; **6:** 23, 28, 66-67, 72-76, 89, 111; **7:** 32, 34-35, 60-61, 69, 83-84; **8:** 32, 49-50, 55-56, 63, 67, 75-76, 79, 106, 108; **9:** 12, 15, 28-29, 36, 42-43, 48, 56, 64-65, 67, 76, 93, 97, 100, 104-109; **10:** 19, 22-23, 25, 35, 48-49, 52, 57-58, 72-73, 79, 90-91-97, 100, 103-107, 109 (See also slavery; civil rights movement)
Agamede **1:** 55
Agassiz, Elizabeth **6:** 93-94; **7:** 27
Agnes of Bohemia **2:** 18
Agnes of Poitou **2:** 81-82
Agnesi, Maria Gaetana **4:** 83-84*
Agnodike **1:** 55
Agoult, Marie d' **6:** 64, **7:** 105
Agrippina **1:** 73-74*
Ahrweiler, Hélène **10:** 57
Aidoo, Ama Ata **10:** 90-91
Aikenhead, Mary **5:** 88
A'isha **2:** 27-28
Akhmatova, Anna **8:** 98
Albret, Jeanne d' **3:** 15*, 50
Albright, Madeleine **10:** 17*, 21, 27, 58
alchemy **1:** 86, 88; **2:** 93
Alcott, Louisa May **6:** 100-101*
Aleotti, Raffaella **4:** 105
Alexander, Jane **10:** 101-102*
Alexander, Mattie **9:** 71
Al-Khaizuran **2:** 31
Al-Khansa **2:** 105
Allgood, Sara **8:** 103
Americas, colonial **3:** 32-36, 54; **4:** 11-18, 19, 21-22, 28, 39-40, 45-47, 63-68, 73-74, 86-88, 94-95, 111; **5:** 10-15, 38-40, 107-108

Ammaiyar, Karaikkal **1:** 98
Andersen, Dorothy **9:** 71
Anderson, Elizabeth Garrett **6:** 65; **7:** 17, 78-79*, 81; **8:** 19
Anderson, Helen **9:** 28
Anderson, Judith **9:** 102
Anderson, Marian **9:** 13, 104-105*
Andrea, Novella d' **2:** 36
Andreas-Salomé, Lou **8:** 94
Andreini, Isabella **3:** 105-106
Andrews, Julie **9:** 103*; **10:** 98*
Angela of Brescia **3:** 60
Angelou, Maya **10:** 92-93
Angeville, Henriette d' **6:** 48
Anguissola, Sofonisba **3:** 107*
Anna Comnena **2:** 35
Anna Elizabeth, empress of Russia **4:** 61
Anne, queen of England **4:** 59*, 60, 71*
Anne of Austria **3:** 9*; **4:** 30, 57-58*
Anne of Brittany **3:** 16-17*, 108
Anne of Cleves **3:** 28-29
Anne Isabella, Lady Byron **6:** 11, 27
Anning, Mary **5:** 93
Anthony, Susan B. **6:** 16, 25, 35, 56-57, 67, **7:** 13, 14*, 15; **8:** 10, 24
antislavery movement **4:** 15, 40; **5:** 44-45, 61; **6:** 54-60, 62
Apgar, Virginia **9:** 72
Applebee, Constance **8:** 72
Applin, Esther **8:** 93
Aquino, Corazon **10:** 12-13*, 21
Aragona, Tullia d' **3:** 65
Arbus, Diane **9:** 111
Arden, Elizabeth **8:** 50; **9:** 46*
Ardinghelli, Maria **5:** 94-95
Arete of Cyrene **1:** 61
Arlington, Lizzie **7:** 72
Armstrong, Anne **10:** 20
Arnauld, Angélique **4:** 16*, 18
Arnould, Sophie **5:** 105
Arrieu, Claude **9:** 107
Artemisia of Halicarnassus **1:** 47*
arts. See visual arts; music; opera; dance; theater; arts, patrons of
arts, patrons of **2:** 72, 100-102; **3:** 96, 108; **10:** 102
Ashbridge, Elizabeth **5:** 40
Ashcroft, Peggy **9:** 102
Ashley, Laura **10:** 67
Asian-Americans **8:** 36, 39; **9:** 22, 37, 39, 43, 88; **10:** 50, 55-57, 68-69
Askew, Anne **3:** 49
Aspasia **1:** 60-61*
Astell, Mary **4:** 26; **8:** 18
Astor, Nancy Langhorne **8:** 19, 26*
astronomy **2:** 35, 93, 97; **4:** 84-85, 87, 90-93; **6:** 92, 94; **7:** 88-89; **8:** 88; **9:** 79-80; **10:** 85
Athaliah **1:** 39
Athena **1:** 56-58*
Atkinson, Ti-Grace **10:** 35*, 37
Atwood, Margaret **10:** 93*
Auclert, Hubertine **7:** 18
Audrey (Ethelreda), St. **2:** 13
Auerbach, Beatrice **9:** 45
Auerbach, Charlotte **9:** 78

Augsburg, Anita **8:** 17; **9:** 11
Augustus, Caesar **1:** 73-77
Aung San Suu Kyi **10:** 11-12*, 21
Auriol, Jacqueline **9:** 56-57
Austen, Jane **5:** 47, 98, 100-101*; **10:** 100
Australia **1:** 91; **5:** 74, 78-79; **6:** 14, 18, 46, 48; **7:** 18, 28, 82, 101, 102-103; **8:** 11, 13, 19, 99; **9:** 21, 64, 102, 106; **10:** 27, 40, 53, 56-57, 59, 61, 75, 108
aviation and space **5:** 80; **8:** 74-76; **9:** 22, 55-58, 81; **10:** 62-65
Axis Sally (Mildred Gillars) **9:** 22-23*
Ayer, Harriet Hubbard **7:** 42, 43
Aylward, Gladys **8:** 69
Ayres, Anne **6:** 87
Ayres, Mary **7:** 41
Ayrton, Hertha Marks **8:** 91*

B

Ba, Mariama **10:** 90
Bacall, Lauren **10:** 102
Bacewicz, Grazyna **9:** 107
Bache, Sarah Franklin **5:** 23-24, 30
Baez, Joan **10:** 105-106
Bagley, Sarah **6:** 33
Bai, Lakshmi **6:** 68
Bai, Mira **3:** 100
Bailey, Florence **8:** 93
Bailey, Mary **8:** 76
Baillie, Joanna **5:** 101
Bajer, Matilde **7:** 18
Baker, Josephine (performer) **8:** 108; **9:** 104
Baker, Josephine (physician) **8:** 78-79
Balas, Iolanda **10:** 72
Balch, Emily **8:** 32
Baldwin, Anna **6:** 95
Baldwin, Mary **6:** 31
Ball, Lucille **9:** 100-101*
Ballinger, Margaret **10:** 25
Ban Zhao **1:** 95
Bandaranaike, Sirimavo **10:** 10, 19, 21
Bang, Nina **8:** 19
Barbie **9:** 46; **10:** 69
Barnett, Margaret Ross **10:** 57-58
Barry, Elizabeth **4:** 98
Barry, James (Miranda Stuart) **5:** 85
Barry, Leonora **7:** 44
Barrymore, Ethel **6:** 105
Barton, Clara **7:** 15, 86-87*
Bascom, Florence **7:** 30, 91, 93
baseball **7:** 9; **9:** 63, 65; **10:** 71
basketball **8:** 73; **10:** 71, 74-75
Bassi, Laura **4:** 84*
Bates, Daisy **9:** 29*
Bathildis **2:** 11, 33
Batten, Jean **9:** 56
Bauer, Marion **9:** 107
Bauld, Alison **10:** 108
Beach, Amy **7:** 104-105, 111; **8:** 108
Beale, Dorothea **6:** 31-32*; **7:** 26
Beals, Jessie Tarbox **8:** 111
Beard, Mary **8:** 58
Beaufort, Margaret **3:** 62-63*
Beaux, Cecilia **7:** 110

Beccari, Gualberta **7:** 18
Becker, Lydia **6:** 94; **7:** 17
Beech, Olive **9:** 58*
Beecher, Catharine **5:** 49; **6:** 15, 26, 29, 40-41, 58; **7:** 16, 53
Beers, Ethel Lynn **6:** 101
Beeton, Isabella **6:** 40
Behn, Aphra **4:** 92-93*, 98
Béjart, Armande **4:** 100
Béjart, Madeleine **4:** 99-100
Bell, Jocelyn **10:** 85
Bell, Laura **6:** 12
Bell, Vanessa **8:** 99, 110
Bellincioni, Gemma **7:** 103
Benedict, St. **2:** 11, 33
Benedict, Ruth **9:** 82-83
Benetton, Giuliana **9:** 45
Bennett, Louise **8:** 46
Berenson, Senda **6:** 72-73
Bergman, Ingrid **9:** 96
Bernadette, St. **6:** 24
Bernhardt, Sarah **7:** 106-107*; **8:** 100
Berry, Mary **5:** 50
Besant, Annie **7:** 51; **8:** 26-27*
Bethune, Joanne **5:** 49
Bethune, Louise **7:** 109
Bethune, Mary **8:** 56-57*; **9:** 12*, 15
Bhutto, Benazir **10:** 12-13*, 21
Bibi Khanym **2:** 31*
Bichier des Ages, Jeanne-Elisabeth **6:** 24
Biheron, Marie **5:** 87
Bijns, Anna **3:** 61, 72
biology **2:** 93; **4:** 87-88; **6:** 93-94; **7:** 27, 30, 92-94; **8:** 91, 93; **9:** 78-79, 81-82; **10:** 84-87
Birney, Alice McLellan **7:** 32-33
birth control **1:** 27; **7:** 39; **8:** 85-87; **9:** 74-76; **10:** 78-83
Bishop, Elizabeth **9:** 94
Bishop, Isabella Bird **7:** 74; **8:** 74
Black, Clementina **7:** 45
Blackwell, Antoinette Brown **6:** 23*, 62, 79
Blackwell, Elizabeth **6:** 25, 53, 78-79*, 82, 88; **7:** 77-78
Blackwell, Emily **6:** 79, 80
Blanchard, Helen Augusta **7:** 95
Blanchard, Marie Sophie **5:** 80*
Blanche of Castile **2:** 77*
Blankers-Koen, Fanny **9:** 64
Blatch, Harriot Stanton **7:** 70*; **8:** 10*
Blavatsky, Helena **7:** 50-51*
Bleibtrey, Ethelda **8:** 71
Blodgett, Katherine **9:** 78*, 80-81
Blond, Elizabeth Le **8:** 74
Bloomer, Amelia **6:** 16, 18, 45
Blow, Susan Elizabeth **7:** 31
Blunt, Anne King **6:** 11; **7:** 74
Bly, Nellie **7:** 43*
Bocage, Madame du **4:** 101; **5:** 100
Bocchi, Dorotea **2:** 77*
Bodichon, Barbara Leigh-Smith **6:** 31, 34, 51, 65, 100; **8:** 18
Boivin, Marie **5:** 85
Boleyn, Anne **3:** 20, 28*
Bondfield, Margaret **7:** 45; **8:** 19, 45-46*

Bonheur, Rosa **6:** 110-111*
Bonner, Yelena **10:** 28
Bonney, Anne **4:** 44-47*
Booth, Catherine **7:** 46-47*; **8:** 59
Booth, Catherine Bramwell **8:** 60
Booth, Evangeline **7:** 47; **8:** 60*
Boothroyd, Betty **10:** 15*, 21
Borden, Amanda **10:** 70*
Borgia, Lucrezia **3:** 39-40*
Bose, Abala Das **8:** 56
Bouboulina, Laskarina **5:** 35
Boucherett, Jessie **6:** 34, 65
Boulanger, Nadia **8:** 108; **9:** 107
Bourgeois, Louise **10:** 111
Bourgeois, Louyse **4:** 77-78
Bourke-White, Margaret **9:** 1*, 110-111
Bowser, Mary Elizabeth **6:** 75
Boxer, Barbara **10:** 21
Boyd, Belle **6:** 74
Bracegirdle, Anne **4:** 98
Braddon, Mary Elizabeth **7:** 101
Bradstreet, Anne **4:** 94-95
Bradwell, Myra **6:** 70; **7:** 19
Bragg, Elizabeth **7:** 90
Bragg, Mary Adela **8:** 88
Brandy **10:** 103*
Brant, Molly **5:** 23
Brassempouy Lady **1:** 13*
Braun, Carol Moseley **10:** 18*, 21-22
Breckenridge, Myra **8:** 81
Breckinridge, Sophonisba **8:** 53*
Bremer, Frederika **6:** 99
Brent, Margaret **4:** 55
Breteuil, Gabrielle-Emilie de **4:** 82-83*
Brewer, Lucy **5:** 31
Brewer, Margaret **10:** 29*
Brice, Fanny **8:** 107; **9:** 97*
Bridget, St. **2:** 20-21*; **3:** 95-96*
Briggs, Emily Edson **6:** 19; **7:** 43
Brigid of Kildare **1:** 84
Brinvilliers, Marquise de **4:** 48*
Britain **4:** 11, 13-14, 18, 22, 26-28, 30-31, 35, 41-43, 47, 51-54, 60, 76-80, 82, 92, 96, 97-101; **5:** 10-15, 17, 31, 38-40, 45, 71, 73, 75, 85, 91, 93. 95, 98-104; **6:** 11-13, 15, 19-22, 27, 31-35, 51-52, 65, 69, 79. 92-94, 98-101, 103-105; **7:** 11-12, 17-18, 19, 22, 26, 35, 37-39, 43, 45, 46-47, 61, 70-74, 77-82, 98, 107-108; **8:** 12-19, 25-27, 44-46, 48, 57, 72-76, 83, 88-89, 91, 94, 98-99, 103, 107-108, 110; **9:** 9, 20-21, 25, 29-30, 36-39, 42-43, 56, 58, 73-79, 82-84, 90-91, 102-103, 107, 109-110 **10:** 10-11, 15, 20-21, 27-28, 39, 41, 53, 56, 61, 64-67, 73, 85-88, 93-95, 100-102, 108-111 (See also England)
Britton, Elizabeth **7:** 94
Brontë, Anne **6:** 98-99
Brontë, Charlotte **6:** 25, 98-99*
Brontë, Emily **6:** 98-99
Brooks, Caroline **7:** 111
Brooks, Romaine **8:** 110
Brown, Olympia **6:** 23*
Brown, Rachel Fuller **9:** 79
Brown, Willa **9:** 56*
Browner, Carol **10:** 8 7
Browning, Elizabeth Barrett **6:** 101
Brundtland, Gro Harlem **10:** 14, 20
Bryan, Margaret **5:** 95
Bryant, Alice **8:** 83
Bryant, Louise **8:** 49
Buck, Pearl **9:** 92-93*
Buckland, Mary **6:** 93
Buffet, Marguerite **4:** 27-28
Burbidge, Margaret **10:** 85
Burdett-Coutts, Angela **6:** 12-14*

Burke, Mary **7:** 44
Burke, Selma **9:** 12*
Burleigh, Celia **7:** 48
Burnett, Frances Hodgson **7:** 101*
Burney, Fanny **5:** 98-99
Burns, Lucy **8:** 19
Burrows, Eva **10:** 59
Burton, Isabel Arundell **7:** 74
business, women in **1:** 31, 33-34, 48, 70; **2:** 67-68; **3:** 70-71; **4:** 55; **5:** 73-74; **6:** 35; **7:** 41-42, 67; **8:** 40-41, 47-50; **9:** 44-47; **10:** 49-53 (See also work, women and)
Butcher, Susan **10:** 76
Butler, Josephine **6:** 12; **7:** 39
Butler, Selena Sloan **8:** 56
Butler-Sloss, Elizabeth **10:** 21
Butterick, Eleanor **6:** 44
Byron, Ada **6:** 11, 92-93

C

Cabrini, Francesca **7:** 47
Caccini, Francesca **4:** 104
Calamity Jane **7:** 67*
Caldicott, Helen **10:** 27
Caldwell, Sarah **10:** 107
Calenda, Constanza **3:** 86
Californice, Rosa **5:** 17
Calkins, May Whiton **8:** 58, 94
Callas, Maria **9:** 104*, 106
Calvin, John **3:** 48-50
Camargo, Marie de **4:** 102-103*; **5:** 107*
Cameron, Julia **6:** 111; **7:** 108
Cammermeyer, Margarethe **10:** 31
Campbell, Kim **10:** 15, 21
Campbell, Mrs. Patrick **7:** 108; **8:** 103*
Campion, Jane **10:** 99
Canada **4:** 16; **5:** 30-31, 85, 99; **6:** 14, 59-60; **7:** 38, 53, 77, 85; **8:** 13, 19, 83; **9:** 21, 53, 80, 94; **10:** 15, 20-21, 53, 56, 93, 106
Cannon, Annie Jump **8:** 88*
Cantor, Barbara **10:** 61
Caraway, Hattie Wyatt **9:** 16; **10:** 19
Carey, Mariah **10:** 107
Carpenter, Iris **9:** 52*
Carpenter, Mary (reformer) **6:** 11, 27
Carpenter, Mary (inventor) **7:** 95
Carriera, Rosalba **4:** 108*
Carroll, Annie **8:** 58
Carson, Rachel **10:** 86-87*
Carter, Ann Shaw **9:** 56
Carter, Elizabeth **5:** 49
Caslavska, Vera **10:** 72
Cassatt, Mary **7:** 109-110
Castle, Barbara **9:** 29-30
Cather, Willa **8:** 97*
Catherine I, empress of Russia **4:** 61
Catherine II, empress of Russia **5:** 9*, 18-19*, 21
Catherine de Médicis **2:** 102; **3:** 1*, 10-11*, 13-15*, 30, 39, 50-51, 74, 78, 97-98, 106, 108
Catherine of Alexandria **2:** 6*, 17*, 100*
Catherine of Aragon **3:** 22, 27-28*
Catherine of Bologna **3:** 42
Catherine of Brunswick **3:** 81
Catherine of Genoa **3:** 44
Catherine of Siena **3:** 19-20*; **3:** 43, **4:** 17*
Caton-Thompson, Gertrude **8:** 93
Catt, Carrie Chapman **8:** 10-11*
Cavalieri, Katharine **5:** 105
Cavell, Edith **8:** 30*
Cavendish, Margaret **4:** 95-96*
Cecilia, St. **1:** 81-82
Cellier, Elizabeth **4:** 79
Centlivre, Susannah **4:** 98*
Cerrito, Fanny **6:** 106-107

Céu, Violante do **4:** 101
Chadwick, Florence **9:** 64
Chaminade, Cécile **7:** 104
Chamorro, Violeta **10:** 15
Champmeslé, Madame **4:** 100
Chanel, Coco **8:** 69-70*
Chantal, Baroness de **4:** 18
Chapelle, Maria Louise La **5:** 85-86
Charles II, king of England **4:** 42, 60, 96, 97-98
Chapman, Maria Weston **6:** 18, 54, 56
Chapman, Tracy **10:** 105*
Charnaud, Stella **9:** 38
Chase, Agnes Mears **8:** 91
chemistry **7:** 30, 92; **8:** 91; **9:** 78; **10:** 85
Chen Lu **10:** 74*
Chiang Kai-shek, Madame **8:** 26-27; **9:** 16-17*
Chicago, Judy **10:** 111
Child, Lydia Maria **5:** 58; **6:** 18-19*
childbirth **1:** 26-27, 52-55; **2:** 90, 96-98; **3:** 80-82; **4:** 76-81; **6:** 84-85; **10:** 81 (See also midwives and obstetricians)
China **1:** 90, 94-96; **2:** 22-24, 60, 62-64, 70-72, 90, 101, 104, 108-110; **3:** 54, 90, 95, 102; **4:** 36, 44; **6:** 22, 68-69, 105; **7:** 22-23, 48, 74; **8:** 13, 20, 26-27, 39, 69; **9:** 10-11, 16-17, 25-26, 33, 41, 47, 68, 88; **10:** 13 14, 57, 68-69, 74, 82-83, 107-108
Chisholm, Caroline **6:** 14*, 27
Chisholm, Grace **7:** 30
Chisholm, Shirley **10:** 19, 22-23*
Chojnowska-Liskiewicz, Krystyna **10:** 76
Chopin, Kate **7:** 100
Chow, Amy **10:** 70*
Christie, Agatha **9:** 91*
Christie, Julie **10:** 100
Christina, queen of Sweden **4:** 61-62
Christine de Pisan **3:** 61*, 64*, 71, 94*, 98-100*
Chudleigh, Mary **4:** 24-25, 52*
Chung, Connie **10:** 55*
Church, Ellen **9:** 57
Cibber, Susannah **4:** 98, 105; **5:** 103
Çiller, Tansu **10:** 14*
civil rights movement **8:** 54; **9:** 28-29; **10:** 19, 22-25
Civil War, American **6:** 22, 35, 56-57, 72-76, 83 88-90; **7:** 87
Ci Xi (T'zu Hsi) **6:** 69; **7:** 22-23*
Clare of Assisi, St. **2:** 13*, 17*, 18-19*
Clark, Hilda **8:** 31-32; **9:** 77
Clarke, Edith **8:** 89
Cleopatra (alchemist) **1:** 88
Cleopatra (physician) **1:** 55
Cleopatra, queen of Egypt **1:** 76-78*
Clerke, Agnes Mary **7:** 89
Cleveland, Emeline Horton **6:** 82
Clicquot, Nicole-Barbe **6:** 18
Clinton, Hillary Rodham **10:** 17-18*
Clisby, Harriet **6:** 18
Clive, Kitty (Catherine) **5:** 103
Close, Glenn **10:** 101
clothing and fashion **1:** 12-13, 24, 28-29, 50-51, 62, 71-72, 101-103; **2:** 53-64; **3:** 18-19, 57, 73-78; **4:** 36, 41-47, 51, 71; **5:** 22-23, 42, 44, 65-70, 80; **6:** 42-45, 64, 72-73, 83; **7:** 62-65; **8:** 48-49, 67-70, 73; **9:** 59-62; **10:** 40, 66-69
Clotilda **1:** 84*; **2:** 10
Clough, Anne Jemima **7:** 26
clubs, women's **5:** 22, 32-33, 45, 60; **6:** 35; **7:** 60-61; **8:** 57, 63; **9:** 105
Cochran, Jacqueline **9:** 57-58*
Colbert, Claudette **9:** 99

Colbran, Isabella **5:** 106
Colden, Jane **4:** 87-88
Coleman, Bessie **8:** 75-76*
colleges and universities **2:** 33, 35-36, 91-95; **3:** 61-62, 64, 86-88; **4:** 25, 61, 70, 77; **5:** 39, 50, 84-87, 91, 96; **6:** 29-33, 53, 78, 94; **7:** 19, 21, 26-30, 72-73, 76-81, 85, 88, 90-91; **8:** 32, 57, 72, 89, 91, 94; **9:** 66-68, 71-73, 79, 81, 83-84; **10:** 30-31, 56-58, 70-71 (See also education)
Colette, St. **3:** 41-42
Collette **8:** 98
Collins, Judy **10:** 106*
Columbus, Christopher **3:** 12-13, 32-34*
Comet, Catherine **10:** 108
computer science **6:** 92-93; **9:** 80
Connolly, Maureen **9:** 65
Conway, Anne Finch **4:** 82
Conway, Jill Ker **10:** 57
cooking **1:** 11, 49, 70; **2:** 37, 39, 85; **3:** 66-67, 69; **4:** 34-35; **5:** 54-55, 57-58, 87; **6:** 37; **7:** 53-54, 92; **8:** 62-63; **9:** 34-35, 43; **10:** 42-44
Coolidge, Martha **10:** 99
Cooper, Charlotte **8:** 72
Cooper, Sarah Ingersoll **7:** 31
Coppin, Fannie Jackson **7:** 32
Corbin, Margaret **5:** 26-27
Corday, Charlotte **5:** 34*, 36
Cori, Gerty **9:** 72[1]
Corinna **1:** 62
Cornaro, Caterina **3:** 108*
Cornell, Katherine **9:** 102
Corrigan, Mairead **10:** 29
Corson, Juliet **7:** 53
Coston, Martha **6:** 96
Coudray, Angélique du **4:** 78; **5:** 83-84
Coudreau, Octavie **7:** 74
Coughlin, Paula **10:** 31
Couzins, Phoebe **7:** 19
Cowan, Ruth **9:** 52*
Cowley, Hannah **5:** 103
Crandall, Prudence **6:** 28
Craus, Henriette de **5:** 57-58
Crawford, Cheryl **9:** 102
Crawford, Jane **5:** 89*
Crawford, Joan **9:** 98
Crawford, Mabel **6:** 47-48
Cresson, Edith **10:** 15, 21
Crusades **2:** 11, 25, 60-61, 75, 77-78
Cruz, Juana Inés de la **4:** 18, 27*
Cummings, Marian **9:** 56
Cunitz, Maria **4:** 85
Cunningham, Imogen **8:** 111
Cunningham, Kate **7:** 44-45;
Curie, Marie **8:** 29, 92*; **9:** 78, 85-86; **10:** 85
Cushman, Charlotte **6:** 103*
Cuzzoni, Franceska **4:** 105

D

Dall, Caroline Wells **6:** 35
Dalrymple, Learmonth White **7:** 31-32
Daly, Mary **10:** 36, 60
dance **1:** 27, 30-31, 60-61, 68, 91, 96, 97-98; **2:** 100-102, 106-111; **3:** 101-103, 106; **4:** 102-103; **5:** 60, 102, 104-111; **6:** 106-107; **7:** 102, 103-105; **8:** 106-109; **9:** 108-109; **10:** 108-109
Dare, Virginia **3:** 36
Darrah, Lydia **5:** 29
Darwell, Jane **9:** 97
Dashkova, Ekaterina Romanovna **5:** 21
Daubie, Julie-Victoire **6:** 32; **7:** 28
David-Neel, Alexandra **8:** 74
Davies, Emily **6:** 32, 65; **7:** 26; **8:** 15, 18

Davis, Bette **9**: 97-98*
Davis, Paulina **6**: 62, 68
Davison, Emily Wilding **8**: 14-15
Dawes, Dominique **10**: 70*
Day, Dorothy **9**: 67-68
de Beauvoir, Simone **9**: 26*; **10**: 19, 32*
Deborah **1**: 36-37*
De Brie, Mlle. **4**: 100
Deffand, Madame du **5**: 51
De Generes, Ellen **10**: 100*
De Larrocha, Alicia **10**: 108
Deledda, Grazia **8**: 96
Del Rio, Dolores **9**: 100
De Luna, Aurelia **7**: 18
de Mille, Agnes **9**: 109*
Demorest, Ellen **6**: 44; **7**: 42
Dench, Judi **10**: 102
Deneuve, Catherine **10**: 100-101
Denman, Gertrude **8**: 57; **9**: 38, 75
Dennett, Mary **8**: 86-87
Depression **9**: 10, 13-16, 27-28, 31-34, 39, 95, 110-111
Deraismes, Maria **6**: 64; **7**: 18
Dern, Laura **10**: 102*
Deroin, Jeanne **6**: 53, 64
Desjardins, Marie **4**: 101
Destin, Emmy **8**: 106-107
Deutsch, Helene **8**: 94
Devers, Gail **10**: 73
Dewhurst, Colleen **10**: 102
Dexter, Caroline **6**: 18
Diana, Princess **10**: 41*
Diana da Ponti **3**: 106
Diane de Poitiers **3**: 108-109*
Dick, Gladys **8**: 80
Dickinson, Anna **6**: 57
Dickinson, Emily **7**: 98-100*
Dickinson, Frances **5**: 41
Didion, Joan **10**: 95
Dido **1**: 40
Dietrich, Amalie Nelle **7**: 94
Dietrich, Marlene **9**: 95*, 100
Digby (El Mezrab), Jane **6**: 48
Dilke, Emily **7**: 45
Dinesen, Isak **9**: 94
Diotima of Mantinea **1**: 61
divorce **1**: 25, 45, 69, 93; **2**: 12, 45, 49, 51-52; **4**: 53; **5**: 14, 36; **6**: 16, 48, 51-52; **7**: 12; **10**: 40, 45
Dix, Dorothea **5**: 49; **6**: 10-11, 88-89*
Dmitrieva, Elizabeth **7**: 23
Dod, Lottie (Charlotte) **7**: 72; **8**: 73
Doi, Takako **10**: 21
Dole, Elizabeth **10**: 48*
Donne, Maria Dalle **5**: 86
Donovan, Marion **9**: 46
Dorothea, St. **1**: 81
Douglas (Chambers), Dorothea **8**: 73
Douglas, Helen Gahagan **9**: 28
Dove, Rita **10**: 95
dowry **1**: 34, 45, 69, 93; **2**: 45-49, 51-52; **3**: 67; **10**: 45
Drabble, Margaret **10**: 94
Drew, Louisa Lane **6**: 105
Drexel, Mary Katharine **7**: 48
Drusilla Livia **1**: 73
Dubroff, Jessica **10**: 65
Duckering, Florence **8**: 83
Dudley, Gertrude **8**: 73
Dugdale, Henrietta **7**: 18
Dumée, Jeanne **4**: 87
Duncan, Geillis **3**: 58
Duncan, Isadora **8**: 106, 109
Dunham, Katherine **9**: 109
Duniway, Abigail Scott **7**: 16
Dunne, Irene **9**: 99-100
Dunning (Barringer), Emily **8**: 83

Du Pré, Jacqueline **10**: 108
Durack, Fanny **8**: 72
Durand, Marguerite **7**: 101
Duras, Marguerite **10**: 90, 94-95
Durocher, Marie **6**: 78
Duse, Eleanora **7**: 107*; **8**: 100
Dutton, Bertha **9**: 83*
Dworkin, Andrea **10**: 37-38
Dyer, Mary **4**: 14-15
Dymphna, St. **2**: 86

E

Earhart, Amelia **8**: 76*; **9**: 55-56*
Early, Penny Ann **10**: 74
Eastman, Linda **8**: 58
Eaves, Elsie **8**: 90
Eberhardt, Isabelle **7**: 74
Eddy, Mary Baker **7**: 50*; **8**: 60
Edelman, Marian Wright **10**: 46
Ederle, Gertrude **8**: 72*
Edgerton, Winifred **7**: 30
Edgeworth, Maria **5**: 98
Edmonds, Sarah **6**: 72
Edson, Fanny **8**: 93
Edson, Temperance P. **6**: 96
education **1**: 21, 31, 61-62, 85-88, 95, 97; **2**: 16, 24, 30, 32-36, 89-95; **3**: 51-52, 59-65, 71; **4**: 16, 18, 23-28, 51, 54, 59; **5**: 46-50, 64, 91; **6**: 25-32, 92; **7**: 26-33, 72; **8**: 55-58; **9**: 66-68; **10**: 20, 56-58, 70-71 (See also colleges and universities; libraries; salons)
Egypt **1**: 17, 21-33, 25, 30-33, 85-88, 91; **8**: 13, 84
Eilberg, Amy **10**: 61
Ekken, Kaibara **4**: 27
Eldening, Grace **9**: 71
Elders, Joycelyn **10**: 79-80*
Eleanor of Aquitaine **2**: 74-77*, 102
Elion, Gertrude **10**: 85
Eliot, George **6**: 52, 98, 100*; **7**: 98
Elizabeth I, queen of England **2**: 102; **3**: 10, 12, 20-31*, 62-63, 65, 82, 97, 101*, 105, 108
Elizabeth II, queen of England **9**: 20-21, 37*; **10**: 10*
Elizabeth, queen mother **9**: 20-21*
Elizabeth of Bohemia **4**: 82
Elizabeth of Hungary **2**: 18, 20
Elizabeth of Portugal. **2**: 20
Elizabeth of Russia **4**: 61*; **5**: 19
Elizabeth of Schönau **2**: 22
Elliot, Jane **5**: 101
Elliott (Davis), Frances **8**: 83
Elliott, Maxine **8**: 101*
Ellis, Florence **9**: 83-84*
Elmendorf, Theresa West **8**: 58
Elssler, Fanny **6**: 106-107*
Emerson, Gladys **9**: 78
Emerson, Lucy **5**: 58
engineering **7**: 90-91, 96; **8**: 89-90
England **2**: 12-14, 21, 23, 25, 36, 57-59, 74-77, 81; **3**: 10, 12, 17-31, 35-36, 48-50, 62-63, 70, 82, 87-88, 91, 100-101, 106, 110 (See also Britain)
Enheduanna **1**: 34*
Equal Rights Amendment **8**: 19, 21, 23; **10**: 20
Erauzo, Catalina de **4**: 47
Erxleben, Dorothea **4**: 25, 70; **5**: 85
Esau, Katherine **9**: 82
Este, Isabella d' **3**: 108-109*
Estrich, Susan **10**: 21
Etheria **1**: 83
Eulalia of Barcelona, St. **1**: 82
Evans, Alice **8**: 79-80

Evard, Mary E. A. **6**: 96
Eve **1**: 36; **3**: 57*
Evershed, Mary Orr **8**: 88
Everson, Carrie J. **7**: 96
Evers-Williams, Myrlie **10**: 23
Evert, Chris **10**: 75

F

Fabiola **1**: 82-83
Farmer, Fannie **7**: 53
Farmer, Sarah Jane **8**: 60
farming **1**: 9-12*, 58-59; **2**: 39-40; **4**: 33; **5**: 54-56, 63; **7**: 52; **8**: 62; **9**: 38, 42, 47-48
Farnham, Eliza **6**: 10
Farrell, Suzann **10**: 109
Fatima **2**: 28
Fatima bint Ahmed ibn Yahya **2**: 30
Faucit, Helen **6**: 103
Faulkner, Shannon **10**: 5*, 30-31*
Fawcett, Millicent Garrett **7**: 16-17*, 79; **8**: 12
Feinstein, Dianne **10**: 21
Félicie, Jaboca **2**: 93-94
Felicity, St. **2**: 15*
Fell, Honor **9**: 79
Fell, Margaret Askew **4**: 13
Fenwick, Ethel **7**: 84-85; **8**: 83
Ferber, Edna **8**: 97
Ferguson, Elsie **8**: 29*
Ferguson, Ma **8**: 19, 21*
Ferguson, Margaret **8**: 91, 93
Ferraro, Geraldine **10**: 20, 33
Field, Jessie **8**: 63
Fielding, Sarah **4**: 94
Fields, Gracie **9**: 108
Figner, Vera **7**: 24
Filosova, Anna **6**: 13, 27, 35
Finch, Anne **4**: 95
Finnbogadottir, Vigdis **10**: 20
Firestone, Shulamith **10**: 37
First, Ruth **10**: 25
Fitzgerald, Ella **9**: 106-107*
Flagstad, Kirsten **9**: 106
Fleming, Amalia **9**: 73
Fleming, Peggy **10**: 74
Fleming, Williamina **7**: 88*; **8**: 88
Flèsche (Tibbles), Susette La **7**: 68
Fletcher, Alice **7**: 69; **8**: 94*
Fliedner, Frederika **6**: 86
Flügge-Lotz, Irmgard **9**: 81
Flynn, Elizabeth Gurley **9**: 27*
Fonda, Jane **10**: 100
Fontaine, Mademoiselle de la **4**: 102
Fontana, Lavinia **3**: 107*, 109*
Fonte, Moderata **3**: 71
Fonteyn, Margot **9**: 109; **10**: 109*
footbinding **2**: 63; **7**: 48; **8**: 69
Fossey, Dian **10**: 86*
Foster, Jodie **10**: 99
Fowler, Lydia **6**: 78, 80
Fox, Leah **9**: 76
Frame, Janet **10**: 95
France **2**: 10, 13, 16, 18-19, 25, 33-34, 36, 44, 74-77, 81, 84-85, 92-94, 104-106; **3**: 10-12, 19, 24-25, 30-31, 42, 48-51, 55, 61, 64, 71, 74, 76-78, 83, 85, 94, 96-100, 103-104, 106, 108-109; **4**: 11, 16, 18-24, 25-31, 43-44, 48, 50-51, 56-59, 62, 70, 72-76, 78, 82-83, 90-91, 94, 99-105, 108, 110; **5**: 14-15, 17, 19-21, 32-36, 83-85, 87-88, 90, 92, 94-95, 98, 100, 102-105, 108-111; **6**: 24, 27, 32, 43, 48, 53, 63-65, 82, 98-99, 102, 106, 110; **7**: 12, 18, 22-23, 28, 73, 71, 76, 80, 82, 83, 85, 88, 104, 106, 108; **8**: 13, 28-29, 48, 74-76, 82, 92, 98, 107-108; **9**: 10, 17, 19-20, 26, 42, 52-
53, 56, 62, 75, 79, 86-87, 94 , 101, 106-108; **10**: 15, 19, 21, 32, 39-40, 57, 79, 85, 90, 94-95, 100-101, 108
Frank, Anne **9**: 24*
Frankenthaler, Helen **9**: 111; **10**: 111
Franklin, Aretha **10**: 105
Franklin, Jane **6**: 48*
Franklin, Rosalind **9**: 78
Franks, Lucinda **10**: 54
Fraser, Dawn **9**: 64
Fredericks, Pauline **9**: 53*
Freeman, Jo **10**: 37
Freud, Anna **8**: 93-94*
Friedan, Betty **10**: 19, 32, 26-27*, 48
Frith, Mary **4**: 47
Fry, Elizabeth Gurney **5**: 45*; **6**: 10, 87
Fulhame, Elizabeth **5**: 95
Fuller, Loie **7**: 105
Fuller, Margaret **6**: 17, 19-20*, 61
Fulton, Sarah **5**: 28-29

G

Gage, Matilda **7**: 13, 50
Gale, Zona **8**: 96
Galiani, Alexandra **2**: 92
Galindo, Beatriz **3**: 63-64, 86
Galla Placidia **1**: 78
Galli-Marié, Celestine **7**: 103
Gamond, Zoé de **6**: 27
Gandhi, Indira **10**: 10-11*, 19
Garbo, Greta **8**: 96, 101, 103-104*
Garden, Mary **8**: 107
Garland, Judy **9**: 99
Garrett, Mary **7**: 76
Garrod, Dorothy **9**: 84
Gaskell, Elizabeth **6**: 100
Gaynor, Janet **8**: 104-105
Geistinger, Marie **7**: 103
Gemmei **2**: 80
Genevieve, St. **1**: 84*
genital mutilation **1**: 27; **10**: 81-82, 94
Gensei **2**: 80
Gentileschi, Artemisia
Geoffrin, Marie-Thérèse de **5**: 51*
geology **5**: 93-94; **6**: 94; **7**: 91, 93; **8**: 93
Germain, Sophie **5**: 90, 96*
Germany **2**: 11, 13-14, 21-22, 24-25, 34-35, 38, 66, 81, 94, 104; **3**: 40-41, 47-48, 55, 67, 81-82, 86, 94; **4**: 11, 22, 25, 70, 79, 85-87, 101; **5**: 22, 42, 85-86, 92-93, 96, 104, 107; **6**: 27, 65, 78, 86-87; **7**: 18, 30, 32, 90; **8**: 13, 17, 20, 24-25, 28, 51, 89-90, 110; **9**: 10-11, 16, 18-24, 42, 54, 76, 78-79, 81, 84-86, 95, 100, 102, 111; **10**: 16, 26, 71, 74-75, 86, 92
Gibbs, Katherine **8**: 48
Gibbs, Lois **10**: 87-88
Gibreth, Lillian **8**: 45
Gibson, Althea **9**: 64-65*
Gilbreth, Lillian **8**: 45
Gillespie, Mabel **8**: 45
Gilman, Charlotte **7**: 100; **8**: 65*
Gimbutas, Marija **10**: 88
Ginsburg, Ruth Bader **10**: 16-17*, 33
Girardeau, Isabella **4**: 105
Giroud, Françoise **9**: 53*
Gish, Lillian **8**: 101-102*, 104
Glasgow, Ellen **8**: 97
Glaspell, Susan **8**: 102
Glasse, Hannah **4**: 35; **5**: 58*
Gleason, Kate **7**: 96; **8**: 50
Glover, Jane **10**: 108
Goddard, Mary **5**: 74
goddesses **1**: 14-15, 32-34, 52-53, 56-58, 79-80, 89, 98; **10**: 88
Goldberg, Whoopi **10**: 94, 100
Goldring, Winifred **9**: 84

golf **7:** 70-71; **8:** 72, 74; **9:** 63; **10:** 75
Goldman, Emma **8:** 23-24*
Goldman, Hetty **8:** 93
Goldsmith, Grace **9:** 74
Goncharova, Natalia **8:** 111
Goodall, Jane **10:** 86*
Gordimer, Nadine **10:** 91*
Gorman, Margaret **8:** 66; **9:** 62
Gottlieb, Anna **5:** 105
Gouges, Olympe de **5:** 15, 17*, 36; **8:** 18
Gould, Edith **8:** 70*
Gournay, Marie le Jars de **4:** 26, 31, 50-51*, 94
Graf, Steffi **10:** 75
Graham, Katharine **10:** 54*
Graham, Martha **8:** 106; **9:** 89*, 108-109*; **10:** 108-109
Grahn, Lucile **6:** 106-107
Grant, Zilpah **5:** 49
Grasso, Ella **10:** 20
Gray, Georgia **9:** 28; **10:** 19
Gray, Hanna **10:** 57
Greece **1:** 18, 33, 41-62; **2:** 14, 32, 101-102, 106; **5:** 35, 99; **7:** 18, 31-32, 73; **8:** 813, 4, 93; **9:** 73
Green, Hetty **8:** 50*
Greene, Catherine **5:** 96
Greenhow, Rose **6:** 73-74*
Gregory, Augusta **8:** 102
Grey, Jane **3:** 21-22*
Griffith-Joyner, Florence **10:** 73
Grimké, Angelina and Sarah **6:** 55 57*, **8:** 18
Grisi, Carlotta **6:** 107
Grisi, Giuditta **6:** 107-108
Grisi, Giulia **6:** 107-108
Grog, Gina **7:** 18
Guarna, Rebecca **2:** 95
Guilbert, Yvette **8:** 107
Gul-Badan Begum **3:** 63
Gulick, Charlotte Vetter **8:** 73
Guthrie, Janet **10:** 76*
Guyard, Marie **4:** 18
Guy-Blaché, Alice **7:** 108
Guyon, Jeanne Marie **4:** 16
Gwynn, Nell **4:** 97-98*

H

Hager, Betsy **5:** 28
Hainisch, Marianne **7:** 18
hairstyles and headdresses **1:** 12-13*, 28-29*, 51; **2:** 53-58, 61-63; **3:** 76-77; **4:** 41-44; **5:** 65, 67-68; **6:** 43; **7:** 63; **8:** 68, 70; **9:** 62; **10:** 66
Hale, Sarah Josepha **6:** 20
Hall, Anne **5:** 110-111
Hall, Julia Brainerd **7:** 96
Hallowes, Odette **9:** 19-20
Hamer, Fannie Lou **10:** 22, 25*
Hamilton, Alice **8:** 81*
Handler, Ruth **9:** 46; **10:** 69
Hani, Motoko **7:** 43; **8:** 49
Hansberry, Lorraine **9:** 93*, 97
Hansell, Ellen **7:** 72
Hardin, Lillian **8:** 106
Hargrove, Rosette **9:** 52*
Hari, Mata **8:** 30
Harper, Pat **10:** 55
Harris, Barbara **10:** 59*, 61
Harris, Helen **8:** 68
Harrison, Caroline **7:** 60-61*
Hart, Marion Rice **10:** 65
Hatshepsut **1:** 38-39*
Hawes, Harriet **8:** 93
Hawes, Lydia **6:** 23
Hawks, Elizabeth **6:** 95-96

Hayashi, Fumiko **8:** 98
Hayden, Sophia **7:** 29*, 111
Hayes, Helen **9:** 102; **10:** 96*
Hays, Mary **5:** 17, 50
Haywood, Eliza **4:** 92
Hazen, Elizabeth **9:** 79
Healy, Bernardine **10:** 80*
Hearst, Phoebe **7:** 32
Hcatlı, Sophia **8:** 76
Hebert (Hobou), Marie **4:** 73
Heck, Barbara **5:** 40
Heflin, Alma **9:** 56
Helena, St. **1:** 82
Helfta, Gertrude von **2:** 22
Hellman, Lillian **9:** 94*
Henderlite, Rachel **10:** 61
Henie, Sonja **8:** 72
Henrietta Maria **4:** 60, 96
Henry II, king of France **3:** 1*, 10*, 14, 30, 97, 108-109
Henry IV (of Navarre), king of France **3:** 15, 50-51, 98
Henry VIII, king of England **3:** 17, 20-30*, 39, 49, 82, 110
Hepburn, Katharine **9:** 93, 97-98*
Hepworth, Barbara **9:** 110; **10:** 110-111
Herschel, Caroline **5:** 90, 92-93*
Hersend **2:** 94
Herz, Henriette **5:** 52
Hevelius, Elisabetha **4:** 87
Hewitt, Sophia **5:** 107-108
Heymann, Lida **8:** 17; **9:** 11
Higgins, Marguerite **9:** 52-53*
Hilda of Whitby **2:** 12, 7: 26
Hildegard of Bingen **2:** 16-17, 34-35*, 93, 102, 111
Hill, Anita **10:** 21, 52*
Hill, Octavia **6:** 13; **7:** 38
Hiller, Wendy **9:** 97
Himiko **1:** 96
Hino Tomiko **3:** 71
Hipparchia **1:** 61-62
Hispanic-America. See Latin America
Hitchcock, Orra White **6:** 93
Hitler, Adolf **9:** 10*, 25, 54
Ho Xuan Huong **5:** 101
Hobbs (Taylor), Lucy **6:** 83
Hobby, Oveta Culp **9:** 21-22, 26*
Hodgkin, Dorothy Crowfoot **9:** 78
Hoffman, Malvina **8:** 111*; **9:** 111
Hogg, Helen **9:** 80
Holiday, Billie **9:** 107
Holladay, Wilhelmina **10:** 110-111*
Hollingworth, Leta **8:** 56
Holm, Hanya **9:** 109
Holm, Jeanne **10:** 27*
Hoodless, Adelaide **7:** 53
hooks, bell **10:** 95*
Hoover, Lou Henry **8:** 73
Hopper, Grace **9:** 80*
Hornbrook, Thiphena **6:** 95
Horne, Lena **9:** 100, 108
Horney, Karen **9:** 84
Hortensia **1:** 70
Hosmer, Harriet **6:** 111*
housekeeping **1:** 25-26, 42, 46-49, 64-65, 68, 94; **2:** 37-41, 86; **3:** 61, 66-69; **4:** 32-38; **5:** 23, 54-59, 63, 77; **6:** 36-41; **7:** 29, 47, 52-59; **8:** 62-66; **9:** 34-35,42-43, 46; **10:** 42-45
Houston, Whitney **10:** 104*, 106
Howard, Catherine **3:** 21, 29
Howe, Julia Ward **6:** 68*, 101; **7:** 15
Howe, Mary **9:** 107
Hoyt, Mary **7:** 40

Hrotsvitha **2:** 102, 104
Hsi-chün **1:** 94
Huber, Alice **8:** 82
Hudson, Martha **10:** 72*
Huggins, Margaret **8:** 88-89
Hugonnai (Wartha), Vilma **7:** 82
Humility, St. **2:** 12*
Humphrey, Doris **9:** 109
Hunt, Harriot **6:** 78
Hunt, Jane **6:** 62
hunting and gathering **1:** 8-10, 13, 14
Huntingdon, Selina **5:** 39*, 101
Hurston, Zora Neale **9:** 93*
Hutchinson, Anne **4:** 14*
Hyde, Ida **7:** 30-31
Hyman, Libbie **9:** 81-82
Hypatia **1:** 85*, 87*

I

Ibarruri, Dolores **9:** 17*
Ichikawa, Fusaye
immigrants **3:** 32-36, 50-51; **4:** 19, 39-40, 63-68, 73-74; **6:** 14, 46-47; **7:** 35-36, 66-69; **8:** 34-39, 42, 44, 51, 53-54, 61, 65-66, 82, 87; **9:** 40-41; **10:** 43
Inchbald, Elizabeth **5:** 103
India **1:** 31, 89-91, 93, 97-100; **2:** 23, 29, 31, 38, 62, 64, 101, 110; **3:** 54, 63, 95, 100; **4:** 42, 62; **5:** 13, 16, 67; **6:** 27, 52, 68; **7:** 19, 81; **8:** 13, 27, 56, 74; **9:** 25-26-27, 41, 67, 94; **10:** 10-11, 19, 45, 59-60, 82-83
Inglis, Elsie **8:** 29
Inquisition **3:** 13, 44-50, 56-58; **4:** 17
Ireland **5:** 98; **6:** 46-47, 87; **7:** 89, 99-100; **8:** 13, 17, 25, 34, 102; **10:** 15, 21, 29, 40
Ireland, Patricia **10:** 33
Irene of Athens **2:** 18, 73-74*
Isabel of France **2:** 18; **3:** 98*
Isabella I of Castile **3:** 12-13*, 22, 46, 53, 64
Isabella, Leonarda **4:** 104
Ise **2:** 104
Italy **1:** 62, 85, 88; **2:** 10-11, 13, 18-20, 22, 36, 42, 57, 59, 87, 91-92, 95; **3:** 14, 16, 39-40, 42, 44, 60, 64-65, 71, 73, 78, 86, 105-110; **4:** 48, 83-84, 101, 104-109; **5:** 86-87, 94-95, 102, 106; **6:** 65; **7:** 18, 28, 47, 106-108; **8:** 13, 20, 28, 55-56, 96; **9:** 12, 16, 19, 23, 42, 45, 74, 101, 104; **10:** 99 (See also Roman Empire)

J

Jackson, Glenda **10:** 101
Jackson, Helen Hunt **7:** 68, 99*
Jacoba de Settesoli **2:** 19
Jacobi, Mary Putnam **7:** 76-77*
Jacobs, Aletta **7:** 13, 82
Jacobs, Helen Hull **9:** 64*
Jacquet de la Guerre, Elisabeth-Claude **4:** 104-105
Jadwiga, queen of Poland **2:** 82
Jael **1:** 37
James, Eveline Roberts **6:** 82-83
Jamison, Judith **10:** 109*
Janeway, Elizabeth **10:** 33
Japan **1:** 96; **2:** 23, 62, 80, 101-104; **3:** 71, 102-103; **4:** 27, 44, 99; **5:** 103; **6:** 44, 105; **7:** 16, 43, 63, 99, 103, 107, 110; **8:** 13, 20; **9:** 10-12, 19, 22-23, 26, 42, 85-86; **10:** 21, 68, 76
Jarrett, Mary **8:** 94
Jarvis, Anna **8:** 66
Jekyll, Gertrude **7:** 110
Jesus Christ **1:** 81-84*

Jewett, Sarah Orne **7:** 99
Jex-Blake, Sophia **7:** 78-81
Jezebel **1:** 40*
Jhabvala, Ruth Prawer **10:** 93*
Jiang Qing **10:** 13-14*
Jingu **1:** 96
Jito **2:** 80, 102
Joan, Pope **2:** 14*, 98*
Joan of Arc **3:** 18-19*, 57, 100
Joanna of Castile **3:** 12*
Johnson, Amy **9:** 56, 58
Johnson, Madame **5:** 80
Johnson, Nancy M. **6:** 95
Johnston, Frances **7:** 27, 110-111*; **8:** 106
Johnston, Henrietta **4:** 111
Joliot-Curie, Irène **8:** 29, 92*; **9:** 17, 78, 86-87*; **10:** 85
Jones, Amanda **7:** 95
Jones, Barbara **10:** 72*
Jones, Mary (Mother) **8:** 41*
Joplin, Janis **10:** 106
Jordan, Barbara **10:** 22-23
Joseph, Helen **10:** 25
journalism and broadcasting **4:** 96; **6:** 16, 18, 33, 43, 45, 64-65, 67, 70; **7:** 14-18, 43, 101; **8:** 16, 24, 27, 49, 92, 111; **9:** 16, 20, 22-23, 52-54, 75; **10:** 54-55 (See also writing and publishing; photography)
Joyner-Kersee, Jackie **10:** 73
Judson, Ann Hesseltine **5:** 40-41*
Julia Domna **1:** 76*
Julia Maesa **1:** 76
Julia Mamaea **1:** 76-77
Julian of Norwich **2:** 21

K

Kahn, Florence **8:** 21
Kairi, Evanthia **5:** 35
Kajiko, Yajima **7:** 21
Kanawa, Kiri Te **10:** 108
Kaplan, Nelly **9:** 99
Karatza, Rallou **5:** 35
Karsavina, Tamara **8:** 108
Käsebier, Gertrude **8:** 111
Kasinga, Fauziya **10:** 82
Kassebaum, Nancy **10:** 20
Kauffman, Angelica **5:** 109
Keene, Laura **6:** 105*
Kehajia, Kelliopi **7:** 32
Keller, Helen **7:** 29*
Kelley, Abby **6:** 56
Kelley, Beverly **10:** 30*
Kelley, Florence **7:** 43; **8:** 54*
Kelly, Petra **10:** 16, 26*, 86
Kemble, Fanny **6:** 103-104*
Kempe, Margery **3:** 100
Kendrick, Pearl **9:** 71
Kennedy (Onassis), Jacqueline **9:** 61*; **10:** 18
Kenney, Annie **8:** 14
Kenney (O'Sullivan), Mary **7:** 36, 44
Kenworthy, Marion **9:** 84
Kenyon, Kathleen **9:** 83-84
Khadija **2:** 26-27
Kies, Mary **5:** 96
King, Betsy **10:** 75
King, Coretta Scott **10:** 22*
King, Louisa **8:** 63
King, Susan **7:** 42
Kingsley, Mary **7:** 94
Kinney, Dita **8:** 29*
Kirch, Maria **4:** 85, 87
Klein, Melanie **9:** 84
Knight, Margaret (Mattie) **7:** 95
Knipper, Olga **7:** 108; **8:** 103

Knox, Betty **9:** 52*
Kolb, Barbara **10:** 108
Kollwitz, Käthe **8:** 110
Komyo **2:** 23, 80
Kondakova, Elena **10:** 63
Korbut, Olga **10:** 72
Kovalevsky, Sonya **7:** 90*
Kovalskaya, Elizaveta **7:** 24
Krone, Julie **10:** 75-76
Krpi **1:** 91
Kumaratunga, Chandrika **10:** 10-11, 21
Kusner, Kathy **10:** 75
Kwan, Michelle **10:** 74
Kwolek, Stephanie **10:** 85

L

labor movement **6:** 33-35; **7:** 36-37, 43-45; **8:** 41-47; **9:** 48-51; **10:** 47
Lacomb, Claire **5:** 17, 33-34, 36
Ladd-Franklin, Christine **7:** 29-30
La Fayette, Countess de **4:** 91
Lagerlöf, Selma **8:** 96*
Laïs **1:** 55
Lalande, Amélie de **5:** 92
Lamb, Mary **5:** 99
Lambert, Marjorie **9:** 83-84*
Lamme, Bertha **7:** 90-91
Landowska, Wanda **8:** 106
lang, k. d. **10:** 106
Lange, Dorothea **9:** 15, 32, 110-111*
Lange, Helene **7:** 17*, 18, 32
Langtry, Lillie **7:** 107-108*
Lansbury, Angela **10:** 97-98*
Laskaridou, Aikaterini **7:** 31
Lathrop, Julia **8:** 52*
Lathrop, Sister Mary **8:** 82
Latin America **3:** 32-36; **4:** 17; **6:** 78; **7:** 28, 69; **8:** 13; **9:** 30, 43, 48, 92, 100; **10:** 15, 29, 35, 59, 80
Lauder, Estée **9:** 46
Lavoisier, Marie **5:** 94*
Lawson, Louise **7:** 18
lawyers and judges **2:** 36; **6:** 70; **7:** 18-19; **8:** 21; **10:** 16-17, 19-20, 21, 48
Lazarus, Emma **7:** 98-99; **8:** 34, 37*
Leakey, Mary **10:** 88
Leavitt, Henrietta **8:** 88
Leavitt, Mary **7:** 21
Lee, Ann **5:** 39-40, 43
Lee, Jennie **8:** 26; **9:** 30
Lee, Peggy **9:** 109
Lee, Rebecca **6:** 81
LeFanu, Nicola **10:** 108
Le Gallienne, Eva **9:** 102
Le Guin, Ursula **10:** 92*
Leigh, Vivien **9:** 92
Lei-tzu **1:** 101-102
Lemlich, Clara **8:** 42; **9:** 51
Lemonnier, Elisa **6:** 27
Lenclos, Ninon de **4:** 29, 30, 91
Lenglen, Suzanne **8:** 73
Léon, Pauline **5:** 15, 17, 33, 36
Lepaute, Nicole-Reine **5:** 90, 92
Lespinasse, Julie de **5:** 51
Lessing, Doris **10:** 94*
Levi-Montalcini, Rita **10:** 85
Levin (Varnhagen von Ense), Rahel **5:** 52*
Lewis (Troup), Augusta **7:** 44
Lewis, Edmonia **1:** 29; **6:** 111
Leyster, Judith **4:** 108, 110
libraries **1:** 21, 85-88; **2:** 32-36, 89; **3:** 51, 59-; **4:** 24; **6:** 30, 32; **7:** 33; **8:** 58; **9:** 43, 66-67
Lieberman-Cline, Nancy **10:** 74-75
Liliuokalani **7:** 23*

Lin, Maya **10:** 111
Lincoln, Abraham **6:** 57-58, 62, 72
Lind, Jenny **6:** 108-109*
Lindbergh, Anne Morrow **9:** 56
Lioba **2:** 13
Lipinski, Tara **10:** 74*
Li Qing-zhao **2:** 104
literature. See writing and publishing
Liu Xiang **1:** 95
Livermore, Mary Rice **6:** 19*; **7:** 15
Lloyd, Marie **7:** 104
Lockwood, Belva **7:** 18-19*
Logan, Onnie Lee **9:** 74
Lopez, Nancy **10:** 75
Loudon, Jane Webb **6:** 93
Louis XIV, king of France **4:** 48, 58-59, 76, 100, 102; **5:** 20, 33
Louise of Savoy **3:** 15-17*, 97
Love, Nancy Harkness **9:** 57
Lovejoy, Esther **8:** 30, 79
Low, Juliette **8:** 73
Lowell, Amy **8:** 97
Lowell, Josephine Shaw **7:** 37
Lowry, Edith **9:** 68
Loy, Myrna **9:** 99-100*
Lozier, Clemence **7:** 77*
Lü, empress of China **1:** 96
Lucid, Shannon **10:** 62-63*
Lukens, Rebecca **5:** 66*, 73-74*
Luther, Martin **3:** 27, 39, 41, 47-48*, 50, 57
Lutyens, Elisabeth **9:** 107
Luxemburg, Rosa **8:** 24-25
Lynd, Helen **8:** 58
Lynn, Loretta **10:** 106
Lyon, Mary **6:** 30-31*

M

McAlice, Lottie **7:** 73
Macarthur, Elizabeth **5:** 74, 79
MacArthur, Mary Reid **8:** 46
Macaulay, Catharine **5:** 49-50
McAuley, Mother Mary **6:** 87
McAuliffe, Christa **10:** 63*
McClintock, Barbara **10:** 84*
McClintock, Mary Ann **6:** 62
Maconchy, Elizabeth **9:** 107; **10:** 108
McCormick, Anne **9:** 52
McCormick, Katharine **10:** 78
McCullers, Carson **9:** 93-94
McDouglass, Harriette **6:** 22
McDowell, Anne **6:** 18
McDowell, Mary **8:** 52*
McGee, Anita Newcomb **7:** 80*, 87
McGrory, Mary **10:** 54
McKeaun, Ciaran **10:** 29
MacKinnon, Catherine **10:** 37-38
MacLaine, Shirley **10:** 102*
McLaren, Agnes **7:** 82
McLean, Evalyn **8:** 63*
Macmillan, Chrystal **8:** 32
McMillan, Terry **10:** 91*
McNeil, Claudia **9:** 97
MacPhail, Agnes **8:** 19
McPherson, Aimée Semple **8:** 59-60*
Madison, Dolley **5:** 53*
Madonna **10:** 104-105*
Ma-gcig Lab-sgron **2:** 23
Magill (White), Helen **7:** 28
Mahaprajapati **1:** 99
Maintenon, Françoise Aubigné de **4:** 23, 30, 58-59*, 62*, 100*
Maitreya **1:** 100
Makarova, Natalia **10:** 109
Makeba, Miriam **9:** 108
Makin, Bathshua Pell **4:** 26

Malintzin (Marina) **3:** 35*
Maltby, Margaret **7:** 30
Mance, Jeanne **4:** 74
Mandela, Winnie **10:** 24*
Mankiller, Wilma **10:** 20
Manley, Mary de la Rivière **4:** 92, 94
Mann, Erika **9:** 52*
Manning, Marie (Beatrice Fairfax) **7:** 43
Mansfield, Arabella **6:** 70
Mansfield, Katherine **8:** 99
Manton, Sidnie **9:** 82
Manzolini, Anna **5:** 87
Marble, Alice **9:** 64
Marcella, St. **1:** 84
Marcet, Jane **5:** 95
Margaret of Anjou **3:** 25*
Margaret of Austria **3:** 16-17
Margaret of Denmark **2:** 79
Marguerite, Countess of Blessington **6:** 20
Marguerite de Valois **3:** 15, 50, 97-98
Marguerite de Ypra **2:** 94-95
Marguerite de Navarre **3:** 14*, 16, 50, 63, 65, 96-98*
Maria, queen of Hungary **2:** 82
Maria Theresa **4:** 60; **5:** 18-19*
Marie Antoinette **5:** 19-21*, 33, 109
Marie de France **2:** 104-105*
Marie de Médicis **3:** 14*; **4:** 56-57*, 77
Marie-Thérèse **4:** 56*, 76
Marillac, Louise de, St. **4:** 75
Markandaya, Kamala **9:** 94
Markham, Beryl **9:** 56
Markiewicz, Constance Gore-Booth **8:** 25
Marlborough, Duchess of (Sarah Jennings Churchill) **4:** 59
marriage **1:** 12, 24-25, 42-43, 45-46, 69, 93-94, 97; **2:** 12, 43-52, 62, 77, 109; **3:** 24-25, 72; **4:** 23-24, 51-54, 107, 111; **5:** 10-11, 13-16, 25, 44-45, 62-64; **6:** 50-53; **7:** 10-12; **8:** 36, 38; **9:** 40; **10:** 44-46
Marsden, Kate **7:** 87
Marsh, Mae **8:** 100*, 104
Marsh, Ngaio **9:** 91
Marshall, Penny **10:** 99
Martin, Harriette **7:** 101
Martin, Mary **9:** 102
Martindale, Harret **6:** 19
Martinelli, Angelica **3:** 106
Mary (mother of Jesus) **1:** 81, 83*
Mary, queen of Scotland **3:** 30-31*, 50
Mary I, queen of England **3:** 21-23*, 27, 49-50
Mary II, queen of England **4:** 11, 60*
Mary of Alexandria **1:** 96
Mary of Burgundy **3:** 11-12*, 17*
Mary of Guise **3:** 30, 50
Mary Magdalene **1:** 81
Masako, Princess **10:** 68*
Masham, Damaris Cudworth **4:** 27
Masina, Giulietta **9:** 101
Masters, Sybilla Righton **4:** 86
mathematics **1:** 85-88; **2:** 93; **4:** 83-84; **5:** 91, 96; **6:** 92-93; **7:** 28, 29-30; **8:** 89; **9:** 80-81; **10:** 85
Mather, Sarah **6:** 96
Mathews, Ann Teresa **5:** 41
Matilda of England **2:** 76-77
Matilda of Tuscany **2:** 10, 82
Matthews, Victoria **7:** 34-35
Maunder, Annie Russell **7:** 89
Maury, Carlotte **8:** 93
Mavrogenous, Manto **5:** 35
Mavrokordatou, Alexandra **4:** 31
Mayer, Maria Goeppert **9:** 87-88*
Mead, Margaret **9:** 82-83*

Mead, Sylvia Earle **10:** 86, 88*
Mechtild of Magdeburg **2:** 21-22, 87
medicine **1:** 11, 26-27, 31, 52-55; **2:** 36, 84-98; **3:** 57-58, 80-81; **4:** 70-81; **5:** 82-89; **6:** 78-91; **7:** 74, 76-87; **8:** 28-30; 78-87; **9:** 22, 38, 70-76, 78-79; **10:** 78-85 (See also nursing; midwives and obstetricians)
Meinhof, Ulrike **10:** 16
Meir, Golda **10:** 14*, 19
Meitner, Lise **8:** 29, 90*; **9:** 85-86
Melba, Nellie **7:** 102-103*
Melisend **2:** 77-78*
Melpomene **7:** 73
Meloney, Marie **8:** 92*
Menchú, Rigoberta **10:** 29*
Mendelssohn, Dorothea **5:** 52
Mendenhall, Dorothy **8:** 79
Menken, Adah Isaacs **6:** 102-103
Meno, Jenni **10:** 73*
Mercuriade **2:** 95
Merian, Maria Sibylla **4:** 87-88*; **5:** 92
Méric-Lalande, Henriette **5:** 106-107
Méricourt, Théroigne de **5:** 32-34*, 36
Messalina **1:** 74
Metcalf, Betsey **5:** 96
Metrodora **1:** 55
Metzger, Hélène **9:** 79
Michel, Louise **6:** 64-65; **7:** 23
Midler, Bette **10:** 89*
Midori **10:** 108
midwives and obstetricians **1:** 26-27, 52-55*; **2:** 96-98; **3:** 80-82, **4:** 20, 76-81; **5:** 82-86; **6:** 84-85; **7:** 82; **8:** 80-82; **9:** 74; **10:** 81
Mikulski, Barbara **10:** 21
Milder, Anna **5:** 106
military, women in **1:** 36-37*, 47*, 91; **2:** 66; **3:** 18-19; **5:** 17, 25-28, 31; **6:** 72-75; **7:** 80, 87; **8:** 28-30; **9:** 19-23; **10:** 19, 26-31 (See also spies; peace movement; nursing)
Mill, John Stuart **6:** 65*; **8:** 18
Millay, Edna St. Vincent **8:** 97
Miller, Cheryl **10:** 71*
Miller, Elizabeth **6:** 45
Miller, Marilyn **8:** 107
Miller, Shannon **10:** 70*, 72*
Millett, Kate **10:** 37
Mink, Paule **6:** 64-65
Minor, Virginia **7:** 13
Miss America **8:** 66, 70; **9:** 62
Mistinguette **8:** 107
Mistral, Gabriela **9:** 92*
Mitchell, Joni **10:** 106
Mitchell, Margaret **9:** 90*, 92
Mitchell, Maria **6:** 92-93*; **7:** 16
Moceanu, Dominique **10:** 70*
Moero (Myro) **1:** 62
Molière **4:** 31, 99-101*
Mongols **2:** 41, 63, 79-82, 110; **3:** 11; **8:** 13
Monroe, Marilyn **9:** 100-101*
Montagu, Elizabeth **4:** 30-31*
Montagu, Mary Wortley **4:** 51, 71*
Montespan, Madame de **4:** 42*, 48, 58, 60*
Montessori, Maria **8:** 55-56*
Montez, Lola **6:** 107
Montgomery, Mary Jane **6:** 96
Moodie, Susannah **5:** 99
Moody, Deborah **4:** 55
Moody, Helen Wills **8:** 73*; **9:** 64
Moore, Annie Carroll (librarian) **7:** 33
Moore, Annie (immigrant) **8:** 34
Moore, Marianne **9:** 93
Moore, Mary Tyler **10:** 97*
Morata, Olympia **3:** 64
Morgan, Robin **10:** 60

Morison, Harriet **7**: 45
Morisot, Berthe **7**: 110
Morrey, Dewens **4**: 14
Morris, Ann **9**: 84
Morrison, Toni **10**: 90-91*
Morton, Rosalie **8**: 28
Morveau, Claudine de **5**: 95
Morzwetz, Cathleen **10**: 85
Moses, Anna Mary (Grandma) **9**: 111*
Moss, Emma **9**: 73
Mossman, Sarah **6**: 96
Mother's Day **8**: 66
Motley, Constance Baker **10**: 19, 23*
Mott, Lucretia **6**: 54, 56, 62, 67; **8**: 18
mountain climbing **6**: 48; **7**: 74; **8**: 74; **10**: 76*
Moutza-Martinengou, Elisavet **5**: 99
movies and television **8**: 100-105, **9**: 95-101; **10**: 93-102
Mozart, Maria Anna (Nannerl) **5**: 105*
Muhammad, Prophet **2**: 26-28, 31
Muldowney, Shirley **10**: 76
Muller, Mary **6**: 65-66; **7**: 10
Murasaki Shikibu **2**: 103-104*; **3**: 102
Murdoch, Iris **10**: 95
Murphy, Emily Ferguson **8**: 19
Murray (Lindsay), Lilian **7**: 81-82
Murray, Margaret **9**: 83
Murray, Patty **10**: 21
Murrell, Christine **9**: 73
Musgrave, Thea **10**: 108
music **1**: 28, 82, 91; **2**: 24, 35, 35, 102-104, 106-111; **3**: 101-104; **4**: 54, 104-105; **5**: 60, 103-108; **6**: 106-109; **7**: 102-105; **8**: 106-108; **9**: 99-100, 102-109; **10**: 103-108
Mussey, Ellen **7**: 19
Myerson, Bess **9**: 62*
Myrdal, Alva Reimer **9**: 27
Myrtis **1**: 62

N

Nafisa **2**: 30
Napoléon (Bonaparte) **5**: 36, 51-52
Nation, Carry **6**: 16*; **7**: 21; **8**: 53*
Native-Americans **1**: 90-91, 93; **3**: 32-36, 75, 77; **4**: 63-68; **5**: 24, 30-31, 76-77; **6**: 46, 111; **7**: 66-69, 99; **8**: 94; **10**: 20, 35
Navratilova, Martina **10**: 75*
Near East, early **1**: 11-13, 15-18, 20-40, 42, 51, 91; **2**: 26-31, 60, 62, 108-109 (See also Egypt)
Necker, Suzanne **5**: 17, 45, 88
Nefertiti **1**: 38*
Nesmith, Bette **9**: 46
Nestor, Agnes **8**: 45
Neuber, Carolina **4**: 101
Nevelson, Louise **10**: 111
Nevins, Anna **7**: 41
Newell, Harriet **5**: 41
New Zealand **6**: 14, 48, 65-66; **7**: 10, 28, 31-32, 45, 87; **8**: 13, 18, 99; **9**: 56, 91; **10**: 53, 56, 95, 99, 107-108
Ngoyi, Lilian **10**: 24
Nightingale, Florence **6**: 87, 88, 91*; **7**: 84
Nijinska, Bronislava **8**: 109
Nijo **2**: 103
Nina, St. **1**: 84
Nobel Prizes **7**: 24; **8**: 31-32, 92, 96; **9**: 67, 71-72, 78, 85-86, 88, 92; **10**: 12, 21, 28, 29, 59, 84-85, 90-91
Noble, Margaret **7**: 48
Noddack, Ida Tacke **8**: 90*; **9**: 85
Noether, Emmy **8**: 89
Nogarola, Isotta **3**: 65
Norton, Caroline **6**: 52

Novello, Antonia **10**: 80*
Noyes, Clara Dutton **8**: 81
Nur Jahan (Mihr-ur-Nisa) **4**: 62
Nurse, Rebecca Towne **4**: 21
nursing **1**: 82-83, 100; **2**: 15, 23, 82-88; **3**: 34, 52, 83, 85; **4**: 18, 20, 71-75, 77-78; **5**: 42, 84-85, 87-88; **6**: 80, 82, 85-91; **7**: 36, 76, 79-87; **8**: 28-30, 32, 78-83; **9**: 36, 70, 73-74, 76-77; **10**: 81 (See also medicine; midwives and obstetricians)
Nutt, Emma **7**: 40

O

Oakley, Annie **7**: 67*
Oates, Joyce Carol **10**: 92*
O'Connor, Sandra Day **10**: 16*, 20, 53, 82
Oghul Qaimish **2**: 80
Ogot, Grace **10**: 91
Oi, Florence Li Tim **9**: 68
O'Keeffe, Georgia **8**: 110; **9**: 110; **10**: 110
O'Leary, Hazel **10**: 18*
Okuni **3**: 102
Olga, St. **2**: 10, 80-81*
Olympic Games **1**: 47-48; **7**: 73; **8**: 71-72; **9**: 63-64; **10**: 70, 72-75
opera **2**: 100; **5**: 104-107; **6**: 107-108; **7**: 102-105; **8**: 106-107; **9**: 104-106; **10**: 107
Ormerod, Eleanor **7**: 93-94
Otto-Peters, Luise **6**: 65
Outerbridge, Mary **7**: 72
Ovington, Mary White **8**: 54

P

Packwood, Bob **10**: 53
Paglia, Camille **10**: 38
Palm, Etta Aelders **5**: 15, 17
Panajiotatou, Angeliki **8**: 84
Pandit, Vijaya **9**: 27*
Pankhurst, Christabel **7**: 17-18; **8**: 14, 16-17*, 19
Pankhurst, Emmeline **7**: 17*; **8**: 11, 14-17
Pankhurst, Sylvia **8**: 16-17
Paradis, Maria von **5**: 107
Park, Maud Wood **8**: 21*
Parks, Rosa **9**: 28*; **10**: 22
Parr, Catherine **3**: 22*, 29*
Parren, Kalliroe **7**: 18
Parsons, Louella **8**: 49
Parton, Dolly **10**: 106
Paston, Margaret **3**: 70
Patch, Edith **9**: 82
Paterson, Emma Smith **7**: 45
Patterson, Cissy **9**: 53
Patti, Adelina **7**: 102, 105*
Paul, Alice **8**: 11*, 19, 21
Paula **1**: 82-83
Pavlova, Anna **8**: 106, 108-109*
Payne-Gaposchkin, Cecilia **9**: 79-80*
Peabody, Elizabeth Palmer **6**: 17*, 27
Peale, Anna **5**: 109-110
Peale, Margaretta Angelica **5**: 110
Peale, Sarah Miriam **5**: 109-110
Pechey-Phipson, Edith **7**: 78-81
Peck, Annie **7**: 74*, 93; **8**: 74
Pedersen, Helga **10**: 19
Peeters, Clara **4**: 110
Pelletier, Madeleine **9**: 7 5
Peltrie, Madame de la **4**: 16*
Peneshet **1**: 27
Pennington, Mary Engle **8**: 91

Penny, Anne **5**: 101
Pérec, Marie-José **10**: 73
Perey, Marguerite **10**: 85
Perkins, Frances **9**: 14-15*
Perón, Eva (Evita) **9**: 30*; **10**: 15
Perón, Isabelita **10**: 15
Perovskaya, Sofya **7**: 24
Peretti, Zaffira **5**: 86
Peter, Sarah Worthington **6**: 111
Peters, Roberta **10**: 107
Peterson, Esther **10**: 19, 47
Pettracini, Maria **5**: 86
Phelps, Almira **5**: 95; **6**: 94; **7**: 17
Phelps, Jaycie **10**: 70*
Philip II, king of Spain **3**: 22-23, 43, 107, 109
Philippa of Guelders **3**: 42
Philips, Katherine (Orinda) **4**: 94*, 96
Philipse, Margaret **4**: 55
photography **6**: 111; **7**: 110-111; **8**: 111; **9**: 110-111
physics **4**: 82-84; **7**: 89-90; **8**: 90-92; **9**: 80-81, 85-88; **10**: 84-85
Piaf, Edith **9**: 108
Pickford, Mary **8**: 101, 105*
Pierry, Louise du **5**: 92
pilgrims **2**: 10-11, 22, 27-29; **3**: 54
Pinckney, Elizabeth **4**: 88
Pincus, Gregory **10**: 78
Pinkham, Lydia **7**: 41
Pinn, Vivian **10**: 80
Pippig, Uta **10**: 71*
pirates **4**: 44-47
Pitcher, Molly **5**: 1*, 22*, 27
Plath, Sylvia **10**: 93
Plisetskaya, Maya **9**: 109; **10**: 109
Plunkett, Maryann **10**: 99*
Pocahontas **4**: 64*, 68*
poisoning **4**: 22, 48, 58
political life, women in **1**: 38-40, 73-78, 96; **2**: 70-82; **3**: 10-31, **4**: 55-62; **5**: 18-23; **6**: 50-76; **7**: 10-19, 22-24, 79; **8**: 10-27 **9**: 9-30, 53; **10**: 10-40 (See also individual rulers)
Pompadour, Madame de **5**: 103-104*
Pons, Lily **9**: 104, 106
Pope, Jane **5**: 102
Poppaea Sabina **1**: 74*
Porter, Sylvia **9**: 45-46*
Post, Emily **8**: 66
Postel, Marie Madeleine **5**: 88; **6**: 24
Potter, Beatrix **7**: 93; **8**: 98*
Power, Eileen **8**: 58
Preisand, Sally **10**: 60-61*
Preston, Ann **6**: 82
Price, Leontyne **10**: 107*
Prince, Mary **5**: 99
Procter, Adelaide Ann **6**: 34
prostitution **1**: 24, 47-48, 57, 60-61, 97-98; **2**: 72; **4**: 53, 54; **5**: 79; **6**: 11-12; **7**: 34, 39; **8**: 35; **9**: 11-12, 23; **10**: 46
Protopopov, Lyudmila **10**: 73
psychology **8**: 93-94; **9**: 84
Ptaszynska, Marta **10**: 108
Pulcheria **1**: 78
Pulitzer Prizes **8**: 96-97; **9**: 52-53, 93-94; **10**: 54, 93, 95, 108
Punsalan, Elizabeth **10**: 73*
Pusimi, Vittorini **3**: 106
Pye, Edith **8**: 31; **9**: 77
Pythia **1**: 59

Q

Quant, Mary **10**: 66-67
Quimby, Harriet **8**: 75*

R

Rabi'a al-Adawiyya **2**: 30
Rachel (Elisa Felix) **6**: 102*
Radcliffe, Ann Ward **5**: 98
Radegunde **2**: 11*, 44
Raiche (Noyes), Bessica **8**: 75*
Rainey, Ma **8**: 108; **9**: 107
Rainier, Luise **9**: 93
Raitt, Bonnie **10**: 103*
Rambouillet, Marquise de **4**: 29
Ran, Shulamit **10**: 108
Rand, Gertrude **9**: 81
Rankin, Jeannette **8**: 12, 19-20, 22*; **10**: 28-29
Ratia, Armi **9**: 45
Rawlings, Marjorie Kinnan **9**: 94
Razia Sultana **2**: 31
Read, Mary **4**: 45-47*
Reals, Gail **10**: 31
Ream (Hoxie), Vinnie **7**: 110-111*
Récamier, Madame de **5**: 51-51*; **7**: 42
Redgrave, Vanessa **10**: 102
Reed, Esther DeBerdt **5**: 23
reform, social **5**: 43-45; **6**: 10-16, 18, 91; **7**: 34-39; **8**: 24, 31, 51-54, 78-82; **9**: 15 (See also antislavery movement; peace movement)
Reibey, Mary Haydock **5**: 74, 78-79
religion **1**: 14-15, 21, 24, 30-37, 56-59, 79-81, 89, 96-100, **2**: 10-36, 39, 45, 52, 54-55, 72-74, 76, 84-92, 96, 101, 111; **3**: 15-19, 22-31, 38-60, 83-85, 97-98, 100-101, 104; **4**: 10-19, 23, 27, 40, 42, 56, 58-60, 66-67, 74-75, 82, 97; **5**: 38-45, 47, 70, 88; **6**: 21-24, 28, 76, 82, 86-87; **7**: 24, 35, 46-51, 82; **8**: 27, 31, 59-61, 82, 89; **9**: 67-68, 74; **10**: 6, 36, 59-61 (See also goddesses; Venus figurines)
Renaud, Madeleine **9**: 101*
Reno, Janet **10**: 21*
Renzi, Anna **4**: 105
Resnick, Judith **10**: 63
revolution **4**: 31; **5**: 15, 17, 20, 22-36, 51-52, 86-87, 94, 98, 109, 111; **8**: 17, 20, 24-25, 28; **10**: 12-14, 21, 37
Ricard, Marthe **9**: 20
Richards, Ellen Swallow **7**: 27-28*, 53, 91-93*
Richardson, Henry (Henrietta) **8**: 99
Richardson, Natasha **10**: 102
Richey, Helen **9**: 56
Richmond, Mary Ellen **7**: 36-37
Ride, Sally **10**: 63*
Rinehart, Mary Roberts **8**: 49*
Rivlin, Alice **10**: 57-58*
Robb, Isabel Hampton **7**: 85
Roberts, Dorothea Klumpke **7**: 88-89*
Robinson, Betty **8**: 72
Robinson, Julia Bowman **10**: 85
Robinson, Mary **10**: 15*, 21
Rodnina, Irina **10**: 73
Roebling, Emily **7**: 90
Rogers, Ginger **9**: 96
Rogers, Mother Mary Joseph **8**: 59
Roland, Manon **5**: 36*
Roman Empire **1**: 33, 62-88; **2**: 10, 32, 35, 44-48, 51-52, 59-60, 72-74, 96, 101-102, 107-108; **3**: 40, 47, 101
Ronzi de Begnis, Giuseppina **6**: 108
Rood, Florence **8**: 56
Roosevelt, Alice **8**: 68*
Roosevelt, Eleanor **9**: 13-15*, 105; **10**: 19, 47, 101-102
Roosevelt, Franklin D. **9**: 13-15, 25, 34
Roper, Margaret More **3**: 63*
Rosalia, St. **2**: 22

Rose, Ernestine **6**: 50-51*
Rose of Lima **4**: 17*
Roseanne (Barr Arnold) **10**: 100*
Rosenberg, Anna **9**: 15
Rosenberg, Ethel **9**: 28
Rosenthal, Ida **8**: 69
Ross, Betsy **5**: 25
Ross, Diana **10**: 105*
Ross, Martin **7**: 99-100
Rossetti, Christina **7**: 98
Rothschild, Miriam **9**: 82
Roy, Gabrielle **9**: 94
Royall, Ann **6**: 18
Royer, Clemence **6**: 94
Rubinstein, Helena **8**: 48-49; **9**: 46
Rudolph, Wilma **10**:72 *
Rudkin, Margaret **9**: 45
Ruffin, Josephine St. Pierre **7**: 60-61
Russell, Dora **8**: 87
Russell, Lillian **7**: 103*
Russia **2**: 10, 80-81; **4**: 61; **5**: 18-19, 21; **6**: 13, 32, 35; **7**: 23-24, 28, 87; **8**: 20, 23, 28, 49, 103 (See also Soviet Union)
Ruth **1**: 37
Rye, Maria **6**: 14, 34; **7**: 38

S

Sabin, Florence **8**: 91
Sabuco, Oliva **3**: 64
Sacagawea **5**: 77
Sachs, Nelly **10**: 92
St. Bartholomew's Day Massacre **3**: 14-15, 24, 50-51, 98
St. Denis, Ruth **8**: 109*
Sallé, Marie **4**: 102-103*
salons **1**: 60-61; **3**: 65; **4**: 29-31, 51; **5**: 36, 51-53
Salter, Suzanna **7**: 11
Sampson, Agnes **3**: 58
Sampson (Gannett), Deborah **5**: 25-26*
Sand, George **6**: 42, 98-100*
Sand, Todd **10**: 73*
Sanderson, Mildred **8**: 89
Sanger, Alice **7**: 40
Sanger, Margaret **8**: 85-86*; **9**: 75
Saporiti, Teresa **5**: 105
Sappho **1**: 6*, 62
Sarashina **2**: 103
Sargant, Ethel **8**: 93
Sarraute, Nathalie **9**: 94
Saunders, Minerva **7**: 33
Savonarola, Girolamo **3**: 42*, 44
Sayers, Dorothy L. **9**: 90-91*
Schlafly, Phyllis **10**: 38
Schliemann, Sophia **1**: 51*; **7**: 91*, 93
Schmidt, Auguste **7**: 18
Schneiderman, Rose **8**: 44, 45
Schnorr von Carolsfeld, Malvina **6**: 108
Scholastica, St. **2**: 1, 33
Scholtz-Klink, Gertrud **9**: 10*
Schrader, Catharina Geertuida **4**: 79
Schreiner, Olive **7**: 100-101
Schröder-Devrient, Wilhelmine **6**: 108
Schumann, Clara **6**: 109*
Schumann-Heink, Ernestine **8**: 106-107*
Schwimmer, Rosika **8**: 19, 32
science and technology **1**: 8, 31, 85-88; **2**: 93; **3**: 92; **4**: 82-88; **5**: 90-96; **6**: 90-96; **7**: 27-28, 75-96; **8**: 84-94; **9**: 78-84; **10**: 84-88 (See also medicine)
Scott, Blanche Stuart **8**: 74
Scott, Charlotte **7**: 29
Scott, Margaret **7**: 71
Scott, Rose **7**: 18
Scott, Sheila **10**: 64-65*
Scudder, Ida **8**: 59

Scudéry, Madeleine de **4**: 30, 90-91
Seacole, Mary **6**: 88
Seeger, Ruth Crawford **9**: 107
Sei Shonagon **2**: 103
Seles, Monica **10**: 75
Semmelweiss, Ignaz **6**: 85
Semple, Ellen Churchill **8**: 58
Semiramis **1**: 40
Seneca Falls Women's Rights Convention **6**: 62, 70-71; **7**: 14; **8**: 18
servants **1**: 25-26, 46, 49; **2**: 37; **3**: 66; **4**: 32, 35, 36-37, 40; **5**: 54-57, 78; **6**: 34, 40; **7**: 52, 57-59
Seton, Elizabeth **5**: 41-42*
Sévérine (Caroline Guebhard) **8**: 49
Sévigné, Marie de **4**: 95-96*
Sewell, Anna **7**: 101
sewing **1**: 49; **2**: 37-39; **3**: 66, 70; **4**: 23-24, 37; **5**: 57; **6**: 37-38; **7**: 55, 95; **8**: 64; **10**: 43 (See also spinning and weaving; housekeeping)
sex education **7**: 39; **8**: 85-88; **9**: 74-75; **10**: 78-79
sexual discrimination **1**: 24-25, 27, 32, 36, 43, 45-48, 52, 56, 60, 69-70, 82, 84, 93-94, 99-100; **2**: 14, 24, 48-50, 66-69, 106; **3**: 19, 55-58, 61-62, 72, 82, 86-90, 95-96; **4**: 13-14, 20-28, 47, 50-55, 67-73, 76-81, 84, 92, 94, 97, 106-107; **5**: 10-19, 26-27, 33, 36, 41-47, 46-49, 73, 78-80, 82-86, 90-92, 95-96, 109-110; **6**: 11-12, 15-17, 19, 22-26, 29-32, 35, 45, 50-57, 61-71, 78-83, 89-91, 93, 105, 111; **7**: 12, 19, 26-32, 42-45, 48-50, 70-73, 76-82, 87, 92-93, 95, 100, 109; **8**: 10-19, 21, 23-24, 28, 35-36, 38, 45, 55, 57-58, 59, 61, 65, 69, 71-76, 81, 83-84, 88-92, 96, 99, 102,106-107, 109; **9**: 10-12, 23, 26, 34-35, 44-53, 66-68, 74, 76-78, 80, 85, 88, 95-96; **10**: 19-20, 29-40, 44-53, 56 57, 59-61, 70-72, 81-83, 85, 94, 96, 99, 110 (See also witch-hunting; sexual harassment; women's rights; women's suffrage; work, women and; marriage; divorce; widows; single women; suttee; genital mutilation)
sexual harassment **4**: 109; **5**: 78; **10**: 21, 28-31, 47-58, 68-72
Seymour, Jane **3**: 20, 28-29*
Seymour, Mary Foot **7**: 40
Shalala, Donna **10**: 58*
Sharp, Jane **4**: 78
Shaver, Dorothy **9**: 44
Shaw, Anna Howard **7**: 48-49; **8**: 60*
Sheldon, May French **7**: 74
Shelley, Mary Wollstonecraft **5**: 98-99*
Sheppard, Kate **7**: 10
Shirley, Donna **10**: 64*
Shore, Dinah **9**: 107*, 109
Shotoku (Koken) **2**: 23, 80
Shuck, Henrietta **6**: 22
Shuda bint al-Ibari **2**: 30
Siddons, Sarah **5**: 102-103*; **6**: 103
Sidney, Silvia **9**: 97
Siebold, Charlotte von **5**: 86; **6**: 78
Siebold, Josepha **5**: 85-86; **6**: 78
Silkwood, Karen **10**: 88*
Sillanpää, Miina **8**: 19
Sills, Beverly **10**: 107
Silver, Joan Micklin **10**: 99
Simes, Mary Jane **5**: 110
Simmons, Amelia **5**: 59
Simpson, Mary **10**: 61
single women **1**: 46; **3**: 72; **4**: 54; **5**: 11; **7**: 12; **8**: 35-36; **10**: 51
Sirani, Elisabetta **4**: 107-108
Sisilu, Notsikelelo **10**: 24

Slater, Mrs. Samuel **5**: 71, 95
slavery **1**: 25, 47, 48, 49, 65; **2**: 72; **3**: 32-33, 35, **4**: 39-40, 64, 68; **5**: 31, 45, 47, 56, 61-64; **6**: 28, 40, 54-60, 72-76; **7**: 34, 39, 59; **8**: 35; **9**: 11-12, 23, 40; **10**: 46 (See also antislavery movement)
Smeal, Eleanor **10**: 33
Smith, Bessie **8**: 106, 108*
Smith, Charlotte **7**: 44
Smith, Maggie **10**: 94
Smith, Margaret Chase **9**: 15*; **10**: 19
Smith, Sophia **7**: 27
Smyth, Ethel **8**: 108
Solomon, Hannah **7**: 60-61
Somerville, Edith **7**: 99-100
Somerville, Mary **5**: 90-91*
Sontag, Susan **10**: 94*
Soong sisters. See Chiang Kai-shek, Madame; Sun Yat-sen, Madame
Sorabji, Cornelia **7**: 19
Sörenstam, Annika **10**: 75
Southcott, Joanna **5**: 40*
Soviet Union **8**: 20, 24; **9**: 19, 25, 47, 74, 109; **10**: 26-28, 62-63, 72-73, 109 (See also Russia)
Spain **2**: 23, 25, 29, 31, 35, 77; **3**: 12-13, 17, 22, 24, 27, 32-36, 39-40, 43, 63-64, 86, 107, 110; **4**: 19, 91-92; **8**: 13; **9**: 17, 77
Spalding, Mother Catherine **5**: 88
Spalding, Eliza Hart **6**: 21
Spark, Muriel **10**: 93-94
Spencer, Anna **7**: 49
spies **5**: 28-29; **6**: 73-75; **8**: 30; **9**: 19-20
spinning and weaving **1**: 12, 16-18*, 42, 46, 48-49, 90, 101-103*; **2**: 37-39, 66; **3**: 41, **4**: 22, 35, 37; **5**: 22, 57, 71-73; **8**: 43, 46 (See also work, women and)
sports **5**: 80; **7**: 70-74; **8**: 71-76; **9**: 63-65; **10**: 56, 70-76
Staël, Madame de **5**: 51-52, 98
Stanhope, Hester **5**: 79-80*
Stanton, Elizabeth Cady **6**: 16, 35, 45, 56-57, 62, 66-67, 70-71; **7**: 13-16*; **8**: 10, 18, 24
Stanwyck, Barbara **9**: 96*
Starr, Belle **7**: 68*
Starr, Ellen Gates **7**: 36
Stasova, Nadezhda **6**: 13, 27, 35
Stein, Gertrude **8**: 29, 97-98*
Steinem, Gloria **10**: 20, 33*
Stevens, Lillian **7**: 21
Stevens, Nettie **8**: 91
Stevenson, Matilda **7**: 93
Stevenson, Sarah **7**: 77
Stewart, Martha **10**: 42-43*
Stewart, Susan McKinney **7**: 77
Stinson (Otero), Katherine **8**: 75
Stone, Constance **7**: 82
Stone, Lucy **6**: 45, 53*, 56-57, 66, 68, 79; **7**: 15
Stone, Toni **9**: 65*
Stopes, Marie **8**: 86-87*
Stowe, Emily **7**: 77
Stowe, Harriet Beecher **6**: 15, 58*, 100
Streep, Meryl **9**: 94; **10**: 99-100
Streisand, Barbra **10**: 98
Stritt, Marie **8**: 17*
Strozzi, Barbara **4**: 104
Stuart, Louisa **6**: 48
Suárez, Inés de **3**: 34
Suavé, Jeanne **9**: 53; **10**: 20
Suiko **2**: 80
Sullivan, Annie **7**: 29*
Summerskill, Edith **9**: 9*, 29*, 73*
Summitt, Pat **10**: 68*
Sun Yat-sen, Madame **8**: 26-27; **9**: 16-17*

Surratt, Mary **6**: 76*
Sutherland, Joan **9**: 106
suttee **1**: 40, 99; **5**: 16
Suttner, Bertha von **7**: 24; **8**: 32
Suzman, Helen **10**: 24-25*
Suzman, Janet **10**: 102
Swanson, Gloria **8**: 105
Swartz, Dorothea **2**: 22
swimming **7**: 73; **8**: 71-73; **9**: 62, 64
Syers, Madge **8**: 72
Szymborska, Wislawa **10**: 92
Szold, Henrietta **8**: 61

T

Tabei, Junko **10**: 76*
Tacchinardi-Persiani, Fanny **6**: 108
Taglioni, Marie **5**: 107-108*; **6**: 106-107
Tailhook scandal **10**: 31
Tailleferre, Germaine **9**: 107
Talbot, Elizabeth **3**: 70
Tallien, Thérésia de Cabarrus **5**: 51
Tandy, Jessica **9**: 102. **10**: 98*
Tanguay, Eva **8**: 107*
Tarbell, Ida **8**: 49*
Taussig, Helen **9**: 70-71*
Taylor, Elizabeth **9**: 99
Taylor, Harriet **6**: 65
Taylor, Laurette **9**: 102
Taylor, Lucio King **6**: 89
Teasdale, Sara **8**: 96
Tebaldi, Renata **9**: 104
Teerling, Levina **3**: 110
Telesilla **1**: 62
Temple, Shirley **9**: 99
temperance movement **6**: 15-18, 23; **7**: 14, 15, 20-21; **8**: 18, 53
Tencin, Madame de **4**: 30*; **5**: 51
Teng, Teresa **10**: 107
Tennant, May **7**: 43
tennis **7**: 71-72; **8**: 72-73; **9**: 63-65; **10**: 75
Teresa, Mother **9**: 67*; **10**: 59-60*
Teresa of Avila **3**: 42, 43*, 52; **4**: 18
Teresa of Lisieux **7**: 50
Tereshkova, Valentina **10**: 62-63*
Terrell, Mary **7**: 60-61*; **8**: 54, 57
Terry, Ellen **6**: 111; **7**: 107-108*; **8**: 100
Tescon, Trinidad **7**: 87
Thaden, Louise **8**: 76; **9**: 57
Tharp, Twyla **10**: 109
Thatcher, Margaret **9**: 30; **10**: 9*, 11*, 20, 27
theater **1**: 30-31, 48, 60, 91; **2**: 72, 100-102, 106-111; **3**: 101-106; **4**: 93, 97-101; **5**: 102-104, 107; **6**: 102-105; **7**: 106-108; **8**: 100-103; **9**: 95-96, 101-102; **10**: 96, 98-99, 101-102 (See also movies and television)
Theodora **2**: 72-73, 102, 107-108*
Theosobeia **1**: 88
Thible, Elisabeth **5**: 80
Thirty Years' War **4**: 10, 19, 56, 57, 85
Thomas, Clarence **10**: 52
Thomas, Helen **10**: 54
Thomas, Martha Carey **7**: 27
Thompson, Dorothy **9**: 52, 54*
Thompson, Emma **10**: 100
Thompson, Mary **6**: 82; **7**: 76
Thrale (Piozzi), Hester Lynch **5**: 53
Tiburzi, Bonnie **9**: 56
Tillman, Juliann **6**: 23*
Tituba **4**: 21
Tofana **4**: 48
Toklas, Alice B. **8**: 29
Tokyo Rose (Iva D'Aquino) **9**: 22-23*
Tomasa, Sonia **9**: 52*
Tompkins, Sally **6**: 89

119

Torogana **2**: 80
Torvill, Jayne **10**: 73
Tower, Joan **10**: 108
track and field **8**: 72-73; **9**: 63-64; **10**: 71-72
Trapp, Maria von **9**: 103
travel and adventure **5**: 76-80; **6**: 46-48; **7**: 66-68; **8**: 74 (See also immigrants; pilgrims; sports)
Travell, Janet Grame **10**: 79*
Tree, Marietta **10**: 19
Triangle Shirtwaist Co. fire **8**: 44
Trieu Thi Trinh **1**: 96
Trimmer, Sarah **5**: 49
Tristan, Flora **5**: 14, 79; **6**: 33-34
Trotula **2**: 91
Trubnikova, Mariya **6**: 13, 27, 35
Trung Trac and Trung Nhi **1**: 96
Truth, Sojourner **5**: 40; **6**: 23, 56, 62-63, 67*; **8**: 18
Ts'ai Yen **1**: 94
Tubman, Harriet **6**: 59-60*, 74-75
Tuckwell, Gertrude **8**: 46
Turner, Clorinda Matto de **7**: 69
Turner, Eliza Sproat **7**: 32
Tussaud, Marie **5**: 110-111; **6**: 111
Twining, Louisa **7**: 37-38
Tyler, Dorothy **8**: 74

U

Ulanova, Galina **9**: 109
Umm Waraqa bint Abdallah **2**: 31
Undset, Sigrid **8**: 96
Unger, Karoline **5**: 106
Urania of Worms **2**: 24
Ursula, St. **2**: 11*

V

Valois, Ninette de **9**: 109
Van Blarcom, Carolyn Conant **8**: 81
Van Cott, Margaret **6**: 23
Van de Vere, Nancy **10**: 108
Van Duyn, Mona **10**: 95*
van Hemessen, Caterina **3**: 110
Van Hoosen, Bertha **8**: 83-84
Van Lew, Elizabeth **6**: 75
Van Meter, Vicki **10**: 65
van Schurman, Anna Maria **4**: 25*
Vaughan, Janet **9**: 73, 77
Vaughan, Sarah **9**: 108
Vaughn, Mary C. **6**: 16
Velasquez, Loreta Jane **6**: 72-73
Venus figurines **1**: 14-15
Vestris, Madame **5**: 103-104; **6**: 104-105*
Vestris, Françoise **5**: 102

Victoria, queen of Great Britain **5**: 86; **6**: 68-69*, 84, 110; **7**: 9, 22
Vietnam War **8**: 22; **10**: 28-29, 36-37
Vigée-Lebrun, Marie **5**: 6*, 109-110*
Vincent de Paul, Saint **4**: 74-75
visual arts **1**: 8, 14-15; **2**: 102-104; **3**: 107-110; **4**: 54, 106-111; **5**: 109-111; **6**: 110-111; **7**: 97, 109-111; **8**: 110-111; **9**: 111; **10**: 110-111
Voisin, La (Catherine Monvoisin) **4**: 48, 58

W

Wagner, Cosima Liszt **7**: 105
Wagner, Johanna **6**: 108
Wald, Lillian **8**: 52*, 54, 78
Walker, Alice **10**: 82, 94, 100
Walker, Madame C. J. **8**: 49
Walker, Lucy **7**: 74
Walker, Maggie L. **8**: 50
Walker, Mary Edwards **6**: 42, 81, 83*
Walpurgis, Maria **5**: 107
Walters, Barbara **10**: 55*
Ward, Barbara **10**: 86-87
Ward, Mrs. Humphrey **7**: 18
Ward, Mary **4**: 18
Warren, Mercy Otis **5**: 23
Washington, Dinah **9**: 108
Washington, Martha **5**: 28-29*
Watson, Elizabeth **10**: 48*
weaving. See spinning and weaving
Webb, Beatrice Potter **8**: 25, 58
Webb, Karrie **10**: 75
Weber, Josepha **5**: 104-105
Webster, Margaret **9**: 102
Weeks, Dorothy **9**: 81*
Wei Shao **1**: 95
Weir, Judith **10**: 108
Weiss, Louise **9**: 17, 20
Wells (Barnett), Ida B. **7**: 34; **8**: 54
Wells, Jane **7**: 95
Welsh, Jane Kirby **6**: 94
Wendling, Dorothea and Elizabeth **5**: 105
Wertmuller, Lina **10**: 99
West, Dorothy **10**: 90*
West, Mae **9**: 96*
Wharton, Edith **8**: 29, 96-97*
Wheatley, Phillis **5**: 98*, 100-101
Whitman, Narcissa **6**: 21
Whitney, Mary Watson **7**: 26
Whittelsey, Abigail Goodrich **6**: 20
Widnall, Sheila **10**: 21
widows **1**: 24, 45, 69, 81, 93; **2**: 45; **5**: 13; **6**: 52 (See also suttee)
Wiegel, Helene **9**: 102

Wigman, Mary **8**: 109
Wilhelmina, queen of the Netherlands **9**: 20-21
Wilkinson, Ellen **9**: 30*
Willard, Emma **9**: 49-50*
Willard, Frances **7**: 15-16*, 49, 64
Williams, Anna (poet) **5**: 101
Williams, Anna Wessel **7**: 82
Williams, Betty **10**: 29
Williams, Cicely **9**: 74
Williams, Grace **9**: 107
Williams, Lucinda **10**: 72*
Williams, Shirley **10**: 15
Williams, Vanessa **10**: 106-107*
Willis, Ellen **10**: 37
Willis, Sara (Fanny Fern) **6**: 19
Wilson, Carrie **6**: 33
Wilson, Dagmar **10**: 27
Windsor, Duchess of **9**: 17*
Winfrey, Oprah **10**: 94, 96-97
Winnemucca (Hopkins), Sarah **7**: 69
Winston, Mary **7**: 30-31
witch-hunting **2**: 16, 69, 97; **3**: 19, 50, 55-58, 91; **4**: 19, 48
Witt, Katarina **10**: 74
Wittenmyer, Annie **7**: 20
Woffington, Peg **4**: 98
Wolff, Sister Madeleva **9**: 68
Wollstein, Martha **9**: 73
Wollstonecraft, Mary **5**: 12-13*, 48, 98; **6**: 85; **8**: 18
women's rights **1**: 21-24, 36-37, 46-48, 69-70, 93, 94; **2**: 66-69; **3**: 71-72; **4**: 50-55; **5**: 10-17, 26-27, 33, 36, 91; **6**: 15-16, 18, 50-53; 61-71; **7**: 10-19, 67; **8**: 10-23, 52; **9**: 10-17, 26-28; **10**: 10-21, 32-40 (See also women's suffrage; sexual discrimination)
women's suffrage **4**: 55; **5**: 13, 91; **6**: 61-71; **7**: 10-19, 67; **8**: 10-24; **9**: 26
Woodhull, Victoria **7**: 10*, 12, 16, 19
Woodward, Mary Ann **6**: 95
Woolf, Virginia **8**: 98-99*
Woolley, Mary Emma **8**: 57*
Woosley, Louisa **7**: 49
work, women and **2**: 42; **3**: 67-72; **4**: 36-40; **5**: 37, 71-75; **6**: 33-35; **7**: 40-45; **8**: 28, 40-50; **9**: 12, 18-24, 33-34, 36-39; 44-51; **10**: 19, 42-44, 47-55 (See also labor movement; nursing; medicine; science and technology; servants; slavery; housekeeping; education; writing and publishing; journalism and broadcasting; visual arts; theater; movies and television; dance; music; opera)
Workman, Fanny **8**: 74

world fair (1893) **7**: 85, 104, 111
World War I **8**: 15-17, 22, 28-32, 41, 44, 47, 91, 93; **9**: 77
World War II **8**: 16, 22; **9**: 10-24, 36-39, 52-54, 57-58, 76-77, 79, 81, 86-88, 107, 111
Wormington, Marie **9**: 84
Wright, Frances **5**: 44*-45, 60
Wright, Helena **9**: 75
Wright, Martha C. **6**: 62
Wright, Patience Lovell **5**: 110-111*
writing and publishing **1**: 13, 20-21, 27, 31, 61-62, 90-91, 95, 98, 100; **2**: 15, 23, 32-36, 100-105, 110; **3**: 59, 62-65, 94-100; **4**: 24-28, 50-52, 54, 90-96; **5**: 17, 46-50, 74, 98-101; **6**: 16-20, 33, 53, 93-94, 98-101; **7**: 98-101; **8**: 58, 60, 96-99; **9**: 90-94; **10**: 90-95 (See also journalism and broadcasting)
Wu, Chien-Shiung **9**: 88*
Wu Hou (Wu Zhao) **2**: 70-72, 74

X

Xiang Jingyu **8**: 27
Xie Xide **10**: 57
Xuan Zong **2**: 108
Xue Tao **2**: 104

Y

Yalow, Rosalyn **10**: 84-85*
Yamaguchi, Kristi **10**: 74
Yard, Molly **10**: 33
Yarico **4**: 68
Yeager, Jeana **10**: 65
Yolanda, St. **2**:18
Young, Ella Flagg **8**: 56
Youville, Madame d' **4**: 75

Z

Zaharias, "Babe" Didrikson **9**: 63*
Zakrzewska, Marie **6**: 80-81
Zambelli, Carlotta **7**: 105*
Zasulich **7**: 24
Zayas y Sotomayor, Maria de **4**: 91-92
Zell, Katharine Schutz **3**: 48
Zeng Ziaoying **10**: 108
Zenobia **1**: 75*; **6**: 111
Zetkin, Clara **8**: 24
Zorach, Marguerite **8**: 111
Zubayda **2**: 29, 31
Zwilich, Ellen Taaffe **10**: 108